SECRETS
—FROM THE—
SOC DRAWER

Inspirations to unlock your inner treasures

JULES PRICE

ILLUSTRATIONS BY RAOUL WIDMAN

EAGLE ONE
PUBLISHING

EAGLE ONE
PUBLISHING

In loving memory of Harvey Price

CONTENTS

When SOC-ortunity Knocks

PRAISE FOR SECRETS
FROM THE SOC DRAWER

Secrets from the SOC Drawer shows how fun and exciting this business can be. Jules speaks from the heart what it takes to build a successful business. As you pick up the book you won't want to put it down. It's inspiring, entertaining and teaches what Send-OutCards is all about. Heck, you can be in any business, read this book, and understand what it takes to succeed.

DeMarr Zimmerman, SendOutCards Eagle Distributor

Sometimes you start reading a book that you just can't put down. They are very rare. This happens to be one of them. I've been a successful SendOutCards distributor for over five years and I still learned some great techniques from this book. But the best element of this book is that Jules weaves in her own life experiences to help share valuable business building lessons that are interesting, fun and entertaining. No wonder I couldn't put the book down!

David Frey, SendOutCards Senior Executive Distributor

Secrets from the SOC Drawer is an amazing treasure chest full of "priceless jewels." Jules Price's examples of what to do and what you can expect as you build your business will bring tears of laughter, and it will also bring validation when you begin to experience the things Jules explains in her book—then you know you're on the road to success.

Bob & Betty Ann Golden,
SendOutCards Eagle Distributors, Master Trainers

Secrets from the SOC Drawer is a delightful read, blended with humor, creativity and insightful jewels of wisdom. It is a must-read for all distributors.

Jim Packard, SendOutCards Senior Executive Distributor

Secrets from the SOC Drawer offers the perfect combination of stories that will be remembered and practical advice that anyone in SendOutCards can follow. Jules puts her wonderful humor and wit into each chapter, making it fun and easy to read. I love that she shares her Magic Sentences and other tips, like "listening to life with SOC ears." Jules also speaks to the psychological side of managing yourself and others—an aspect of network marketing that is core to anyone's success in this industry. This book is a must-read for anyone serious about building a thriving team.

Kathy Paauw, SendOutCards Executive

We all want to know the secrets to building this business. What are the top leaders doing? If you are staying connected, you hear the same message over and over again: Simplicity, consistency, time. You are doing the work, you are attending the events, but something is missing. This book will complete the puzzle. Whether it's one of Jules' witty stories that convey a powerful message, or the way she uses her magic sentences and power of words to engage people—you are holding priceless information on building a thriving SendOutCards business. I have learned a lot from Jules, and now you and your team can too.

Adam Packard, SendOutCards Senior Executive
Distributor, author of *Stay the Course*

Brilliant, specific, insightful and funny! Jules Price has just given us a masterful roadmap to SendOutCards success. I almost leapt for joy after the first couple of pages. Every idea, concept, story and suggestion will put you in direct line to create very powerful results in SOC. No more guessing, no more trial by error, no lofty ideals, no grand theories—just practical, pragmatic, concrete suggestions that ANYONE can do. Just read this book, apply her ideas and watch your business take off!

Linda Larsen, SendOutCards Senior Manager Distributor, author of *12 Secrets to High Self-Esteem*

Secrets From the SOC Drawer is immediately engaging. As Jules Price goes through every thought, excuse, or response one may have, give or receive while building their SendOutCards business, I found myself laughing in agreement. Her creative "SOC-abulary" pinpoints exactly what every distributor needs to hear. Jules' personal stories bring out her fun and down-to-earth personality as she describes the valuable lessons she has learned. Her passion for SendOutCards is evident, and it is hard not to adopt the same excitement while reading this book.

Megan Drescher, SendOutCards Senior Manager Distributor

SOCKS

No matter what I do,
no matter how I try,
I always lose a sock,
when I wash and get them dry.

I'm pretty sure there is
a monster trapped inside,
that feeds and feeds on socks,
with a monstrous appetite.

He gobbles up argyles,
he wolfs down woolen socks,
he chews on cotton ones,
he'll eat up any socks.

But he's picky and he's cruel,
he only eats just one,
from each and every pair,
that's how he has his fun.

He makes my socks mismatch,
with all the ones he took,
but what he doesn't know is—
I like the way they look

—*Shawn Forno*

INTRODUCTION

Have you ever noticed that people tend to put things in their sock drawer *other* than socks? It's a place to stash things, to store them away for when the occasion arises—a haven for random yet useful knick-knacks.

In a business such as SendOutCards, the little bits of knowledge that you collect along the way are sometimes the most useful, because these nuggets of wisdom give you a vocabulary of tools and thoughts to draw upon. It is too easy for people to get lost in the "big picture," whereas the little things are often easier to grasp, relate to, and then access when a particular situation occurs. It's more manageable to learn these small lessons along the way, rather than trying to understand everything at once. You're able to actually hear that "mantra" or that "magic sentence" in your head, and therefore have more confidence in your responses and actions.

My intention in writing *Secrets from the SOC Drawer* is to bring to light some important concepts that have surfaced throughout my personal SendOutCards journey. I've learned a lot through my own experiences in the last three years by throwing myself into this wonderful business with enthusiasm and gusto! I've always enjoyed creating magic sentences and catchy phrases with a lesson or idea attached, that will perhaps help others see the humor in a situation or catch themselves in a bad habit.

The concepts serve as your "SOC GPS," keeping you on course, and guiding you on the best and shortest path to your destination. When a detour arises in your journey, which it always does, your SOC GPS immediately and calmly takes in the new information that it's given, and recalculates the best alternative route, without halting your forward momentum.

Think about the navigation system in your vehicle: If you make a wrong turn, does your GPS suddenly sigh really big and say, "You know what? Maybe you don't really want to go there after all. Just forget it." Or, "Oh just pull over and stop, you're totally lost and it's not worth it. Just choose an easier and closer destination." No way! The ever-persistent voice keeps giving you the way, in a perky British accent, no matter how many missteps you make, until she proudly announces that you've reached your destination. What would you have done without her?

My mother had always disliked driving to unknown locations until one day she bought "Nuvi," her new portable GPS that she jokingly and affectionately personifies as if it's a good friend of hers. Nuvi comes on road trips and keeps her company, and Mom no longer minds driving as long as trusty Nuvi is by her side to tell her where to turn. (No, she doesn't sit down and eat with Nuvi, or I'd have to stage an intervention!) But the point is, people are much more likely to embark on an unknown journey when they feel like they have something steady and dependable to guide them.

Your SOC GPS is no different. As you go along, you will hear these magic sentences and phrases in your mind. The sum of those small parts makes up that strong foundation necessary to achieve the success and longevity you need to reach your final destination.

As Jeff Olson discusses in *The Slight Edge*, it's the small things that give you the advantage over time, as long as you are consistently moving in a positive direction.

However, it's not enough to have the magic nuggets guide you. You will also need to have the will to follow the GPS voice all the way through your journey. Even in your car, you could switch it off, and wham, you're no closer to where you want to go, and chances are you'll settle for somewhere else. So in your success journey, you must also factor in motivation, desire, and productivity.

You certainly don't have to work 24 hours a day to be successful in network marketing; in fact, it's the aim to leverage your time so that you can work part-time while you enjoy a substantial full-time income. However, you would be hard-pressed to find a leader in this industry who hasn't worked extremely hard—who doesn't eat, sleep, and breathe their business for at least an extended period of time—to get their business off the ground.

This business is simple, but it's not easy; those who expect money to flow in without applying themselves are going to be a bit disappointed, to say the least. We all have a fairly level playing field with the same tools and resources at our disposal. So why is it that some people are naturally more successful in this industry than others?

This is a business of duplication, yet people need something concrete and clear to duplicate. Think about all the top leaders of SendOutCards—probably about as different and diverse as can be, right? Yet despite these vast differences, they all have strong skills in these three "success variables" that I've identified:

1) The way one tends to *process and interpret* information.
2) The way one is able to *frame things* with language.
3) The way one can then *convey these concepts* to others.

Leaders are able to find a way to frame what they're doing in a way that others can relate to, continually overcome any obstacles, and use language that's clear and understandable, so that others are willing and able to embrace their vision and duplicate their actions.

That's why the magic sentences and concepts illuminated in this book can really make a difference and set you and your team on a clear and strong path. Once these ideas are learned and understood, they can then be stored in your SOC Drawer to use whenever you hit that bump in the road.

Your SOC Drawer is a place to stash nuggets of wisdom, lessons, stories, mistakes, systems, and inspirations. The juicy stockpile of support represents your secret soldiers, your back-up singers, and your best friends on a bad day!

In network marketing, there will be ups and downs. No question about it! And not only do we have to deal with our own peaks and valleys, but by the very nature of this industry, we are inexorably linked with many other people and personalities, whom we are constantly trying to drag...oops, I mean encourage!

Yes, you are not alone in sometimes feeling like you are the head cheerleader for a squad of undead zombies! Much to our chagrin, we can't *make people* be great at something. They have to want it. We can't want it badly enough FOR them. And there will be many people you meet along the way who just don't want it enough. As Confucius says, *"You can't stuff a sock in an unopened drawer!"* (Well, maybe he didn't really say that, but he should have!)

But if you're reading this and you DO want to be great at your business, this book is for you. The nuggets you store in your SOC Drawer can be learned. My goal is to provide a helpful framework to those who **want** to be great, so it might help you achieve a top level of success in your business. Most importantly, you can constantly add to your own SOC Drawer as you go, and help to round out and fill the drawers of others who *want* to do the same.

magic
sentences

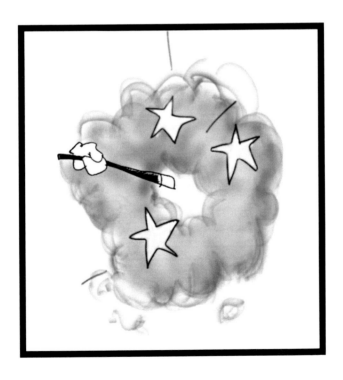

PRACTICAL SOCS

I love creating magic sentences. What qualifies as a "magic" sentence, you ask? Because I said so! No, that's not it. There are certain criteria that a sentence has to embody to transform it from an ordinary sentence into a **magical** sentence!

Criteria such as:

1) It is extremely effective.
2) It will never make you feel "sales-y."
3) It is fun and catchy.
4) It applies in almost all situations.
5) It's duplicatable and memorable.

Most of the magic sentences in this book are **conceptual** snippets, meant to resonate in your mind, and serve as those GPS guidelines we talked about. Other magic sentences are **practical** snippets, designed for you to actually speak aloud, word-for-word, in your prospecting or follow-up.

The practical ones aren't as interesting, but boy, they will be some of the sharpest and most useful tools in your toolbox. Let's warm up with a couple of those to start.

So two of the most commonly asked questions you'll hear in this business are:

1) How do you approach someone about SendOutCards?
2) How do you follow up with someone once you've shown them the tool and opportunity?

If people don't feel comfortable doing **both** of those things, then guess what? They will never share SOC with anyone. Their illustrious SOC career will end before you can even breathe the hopeful words, "Three-way call?"

So here are two magic sentences that address those issues head-on. Interestingly, these sentences will work no matter how you are sharing the system. Whether you're about to show them the automated walkthrough and video, invite them to a hotel meeting or opportunity meeting, sit down for a one-on-one, or do a three-way call, you still need to get them to agree to take a look at it, and you still need to follow up with them after they do.

Unless you're a genius internet marketer who has figured out a way to successfully share this extremely personal relationship marketing tool without ever speaking to another human being, (how do they do it? When's THAT book coming out?) then these sentences will work for you.

So sit back, relax, and prepare yourself for the sheer simplicity of these magic nuggets.

MAGIC SENTENCE #1
Q: How do you get people to do a walkthrough of Send-OutCards?

My magic sentence is:
> **I don't know if you would be interested, but …**

Phew, that went by fast. Let's try that again.
> **I don't know if you would be interested, but …**

"But that's only half a sentence!" you're thinking. Yes, that's true, but bear with me. We're just getting warmed up.

So when you're talking to someone about the tool, you could finish that sentence with:

> "I don't know if you would be interested, but I just started using this great tool for my (real estate) business, and it enables me to (remember clients' birthdays and even send them a cool gift card)."

Say a **few** words about why it saves you time or money or reminds you about things. Then continue with:

> "It could be interesting for your (mortgage) business. If you'd like, I can show it to you. It only takes about 20 minutes over the phone. Do you have a good time this week or next when you'll be at a computer?"

Or when you're leading with the opportunity, you could say:

> "I don't know if you would be interested, but I just started a business sharing this great tool with others, and it has already enabled us to (make a couple hundred dollars a month toward our car payments).It could be interesting for you to maybe take a look at it as well, and see if it's a good fit. It only takes about 20 minutes over the phone and I can show you how it works. Do you have a good time this week or next when you'll be at a computer?"

Okay, so now you are complaining that those are paragraphs, not sentences—yes, I know! But the magic is in the first part, *"I don't know if you would be interested but..."*

And here's the freeing part. You can use that **in any situation:** whether you are talking to your neighbor, your best friend, someone you just met, or to a business owner. It spans all people and all situations. It is nonthreatening and non-pushy. You're expressing that you find something interesting, and asking when you can show them, to see if they'll find it interesting too. Not IF you can show them, mind you, but WHEN you can show them.

I'm always amazed when people say to me, "I have trouble getting people to agree to take a look at SOC." Well, if that's the case, you're probably saying way too much to begin with. The less you say, the better. Don't sit and talk to them for 10 minutes about why they should do SendOutCards or all of the millions of things they can do with it. You don't want to give people a reason to say no before they have even seen it!

DeMarr Zimmerman, SOC Eagle Distributor and the creator of the Fast Start CD system, uses the wonderful analogy of the Valley of Death. The moment you say too much, you will slip off the bridge that would have carried your prospect safely to the presentation, and you plunge headfirst into the dark and murky abyss!

Just don't do it, despite the pressing temptation to blurt out everything you've ever enjoyed about SOC. The more you describe it to someone, the more it is going to sound "hard," which makes people automatically want to say no to whatever it is that you're asking.

Keep your magic sentence very short, and just say one thing about why you like it, one sentence about why *they* might like it, and then ask if there are 20 minutes when they'll be at their computer and you can show it to them.

Maybe not everyone will decide to purchase SOC once they see it, but everyone has to at least **see it**. Why would anyone say, "No, no, I don't want to even SEE something that's out there that will save me time and money and I don't want to know my options!"

And then, as we know, the system really does sell itself when they watch the video and send a card to somebody they care about. So your goal is simply to get them to agree to see it. Don't ask *if* they want to see it. Ask *when* they'd want to see it. You're just being helpful.

Even the grumpiest person, who has agreed under duress to sit through your walkthrough to get you off his or her back, usually can't help mumbling something that sounds a lot like "This is so cool…" Uh, YEAH, I KNOW! Why do you think I've been telling you about it for a month and a half! Sheesh.

So practice the sentence (come on, you can say it out loud—no one's listening right now!) and when you say it, give it the same tone and intent as, "I don't know if you would be interested, but I just found out that Macy's is giving away dresses for $10. You might want to go down there later and check it out."

Now, are you invested in whether they run down to Macy's and buy a dress? No! But you think it is something they should know about, because you certainly enjoyed getting **your** dress for $10!

SOC is simply something that **you** love using, and you would be interested in showing it to them to see if they are interested in using it too. If you use that as your approach, you will never feel like you are selling the system—and they won't feel like they are being sold to, which is even more important.

MAGIC SENTENCE #2

Okay, so you've gotten good at that one. You've practiced the Macy's tone, along with your magical, non-threatening casual sentence, and they've told you that they love it! They say they want to talk to their spouse and thanks so much, they'll get back to you. And then...crickets. You don't hear anything.

And now you have to follow-up. The terror sets in. The palms are sweaty. What if she decided she hates it? What if her husband said no way? What if...well...hmmm...maybe I'll call her tomorrow—or not....

One of the biggest reasons people don't succeed in SOC is they fall down on their follow-up. They do a good job sharing the system, their prospects love it, and then they get scared because they feel like they are "selling" when they call to follow up, so they don't make the call. That's kind of like throwing your hard-earned presentation out the window, because most of the time you'll need to follow up with them or they won't sign up on their own.

So now you need the next practical magic sentence.

After I do a walkthrough or presentation, if they don't purchase a package on the spot, I tell people their gift account is good for six days, but that if they need more time, that's no problem—I can extend that for them. In actuality, I've set their gift account for 60 days in Management Tools, so I don't have to keep extending it for them if they don't make a decision right away. I wouldn't want them to try to go back in to their account and not be able to because it had expired.

But I usually tell them that they have six days, so they won't feel pressured to make a decision on the spot if they're not ready. At the same time, they know they have to decide before the week is out, or at least ask me for an extension. And most importantly, this gives me a reason to follow up with them.

So—back to the magic sentence! Remember, you've told them they have six days before it expires, and if they need more time you can extend that for them. So on the fifth day after the walkthrough, call them and say:

> **"Hi! This is xxxxxx from SendOutCards. I just called to let you know your gift account is going to expire, and I was wondering if you know what you would like to do or if you need more time?"**

Did you feel how awesome that sentence is? It is so powerful because you are not being pushy. You'll never feel pushy saying it, and they don't feel pushed!

And even more brilliantly, when you say that magic sentence and wait for their answer, they'll proceed to tell you what it is that they're waiting for—or what their obstacles are—every time! If you keep your focus on the life of their gift account, they have to tell you when they'll be ready to look at it again because you're telling them that you're resetting their expiration date. So it goes something like this.

They say, "Oh. Well, I haven't looked at it yet and I need more time." You say, "Okay, no problem! When do you think you'll get to it? I can extend it as long as you'd like." And they tell you when to follow up with them. So you will! (More on that in a minute.)

Or, they say, "My business partner is coming in next week and I want her to see it too." So, you say, "Okay, great. Do you think you'll get to it by Friday? Yes? Okay, I'll extend it until Friday—no problem."

So, basically no matter what their hesitation or obstacle is, that sentence will bring it out, and they'll tell you what they're waiting for and when to call them again. You'll be amazed.

So, write it down in your follow-up book, Daily 8 Planner, business card binder, or whatever your organization system is, and then call them again on the day they told you to call.

And NOW, what do you say when you call them back? You say:

> **"Hi, this is xxxxx from SendOutCards. I'm just calling you to let you know your gift account is going to expire, and I wanted to see if you know what you'd like to do or if you need more time?"**

Sound familiar? Yep! You just say that sentence over and over and over again! Whether it takes two weeks, three months or eight years, (let's hope not!) they will tell you when to follow up with them and what they want to do. It is amazing because so many times someone will just say, "Oh, yeah, yeah, I'm ready," and they will almost always thank ME for being persistent and for my excellent follow-up!

So you will never feel sales-y. You are helping **them**. You're calling them when **they** told you to. You're helping them get set up when **they're** ready, not on **your** timetable.

And most importantly you will always know what to say when you pick up the phone to call them because **you always say the same thing.**

The second you have doubts about what to say, that's when the inactivity and excuses creep in. You start feeling like, "Oh, I'm not good at this and they are not going to want it anyway and they're avoiding my calls," and all of that other negative self-talk that is hard to recover from.

So, if you stick to this system and the magic sentences, it will help you be clear about exactly what to say when you call, and they will tell you when to call again! Then when you call, you use the magic sentence again. You just keep repeating that until they say no or yes, and either way you really don't care. You just want an answer either way. In fact, sometimes you'll be hoping they just go ahead and tell you that they are not interested so you can finally take them out of your follow-up book and stop looking at their name!

But always assume they still are actually interested until they say they are not. After all, you're simply acting on the last thing they said, which was "This is really neat," so why would they have changed their mind?

By the way, if you get their voicemail when you're calling, guess what you say on the message? **The same thing!** I promise you. You're just establishing yourself as a business person who cares about your product and business opportunity, and wants to help them when they're ready to start.

Haven't you ever had someone try to sell you something, and after you've never called them back, they've just trailed off and stopped trying? And you actually think to yourself, "Huh! Well, I guess they didn't really **want** me to buy that insurance policy!" Even if you don't want to purchase it, you respect someone who gives weight and value to their product.

It is very rare that they'll ever pick up the phone and call you back by the way, so don't be disheartened if they don't. *Expect that they won't,* in fact. Put them in your follow-up book to try again in a few days. But you still have to leave that message. Don't you dare hang up! Because they need to know that you're still extending their gift account.

If you keep the focus of your follow-up completely about that little gift account, and you're trying to help them out by keeping it alive (while they still have their one little contact and one tiny group and one bitty action log activity), until they decide what package they want, then you'll always **have a reason to call them.** Their account is expiring, remember? You're just saving them from imminent despair if their free card goes away and they will no longer be able to act on their promptings at a moment's notice.

So what happens if you get busy and you don't get around to making that follow-up call when you were supposed to, or it's been forever since you've been following up and you're not connecting with them in person? No problem. Simply change the magic sentence slightly to:

"Hi, this is xxxxxxx from SendOutCards. I wanted to let you know I've been extending your gift account, and I just wanted to know if you know what you'd like to do or if you need more time."

Again, you're just being helpful. They don't have to know that in actuality you were picking up your kids, or at work, or just didn't get around to it! No, you've been "extending it for them." They'll actually be appreciative.

So put both sentences together. In sandwich terminology, the meat is the presentation (however you're sharing it in that moment) and these two magic sentences are the "slices of bread" that surround it. You need all three elements to make it work.

Simply approach people with the magic sentence and ask them when they'd like to see the tool and opportunity. Then after they've seen it, follow up with the other magic sentence, and that's it!

Every day, share the system with someone, and follow up with someone else. If you're consistent with this, you will have people signing up on a regular basis.

knick-knacks and nuggets

DON'T TRY IT; LIVE IT

I went to a friend's party once to support her new travel business, and after the presentation her upline "expert" who had come down from Atlanta followed me around the room for an hour saying over and over, "So Jules, are you gonna *get in*?" until I wanted to karate-kick that smarmy expression off his face!

SendOutCards is not something that you "do." You don't "get in" or "try it." SendOutCards allows you to make an incredible income while using the product daily to build a business, share humor, touch lives, strengthen and grow relationships, and help others. It is a lifestyle, not something that will or won't "work."

It is something you use and in the process, it becomes very easy to refer to others. It works with what you are already doing, and in most cases, it takes on a life of its own. Many of us believe this wholeheartedly: "You don't get into SendOutCards. Send-OutCards gets into you."

Have you ever heard a prospect say, "Well, I like it, but these things never work?" First of all, as you start to read and learn more about the network marketing industry, with incredible books like *The Business of the 21st Century* by Robert Kiyosaki, your "MLM blueprint," as Kody Bateman calls it, will get stronger and stronger! You'll know from the bottom of your little socks that network marketing is a viable and vibrant business model, supported by business leaders across the globe. It's not the company in question or the industry that "doesn't work." It's the individual who fails to follow a duplicatable system, or gives up before he leverages the powerful element of time.

On top of all that, once you truly understand how SOC gets inside people, you can really come from a complete place of confidence and reassurance. What is there to "not work?"

When you send a card, someone gets it in the mail. When you share it with people, you get paid. The checks always arrive on time, every week, every month. As you grow a team, your residuals grow as well. It's a tool that people use every day. You can never lose ground because you can't be demoted. You can do as much or as little as you want.

The MLM structure of the business simply gives you the capability to gain time and money leveraging, enabling you to ultimately make more income than you ever could in a traditional business model.

But even if for some crazy reason you choose to do the bare minimum and never tap into the power of building a team, you can still send great cards and make upfront bonuses when you do share it. Which part of that doesn't work?

Strengthen your own beliefs, and you will find you'll rarely get objections like that anymore. But if you do, you'll be able to share your strong vision and conviction as to why this business is something everyone can feel comfortable entering into with both their energies and their hearts.

The only thing I'm going to "get into" is a state of happiness knowing that I'm making people's lives better. I guess I'd better go send Travel Boy a sympathy card.

WHO WANTS TO PLAY?

Last year I was at the Treat'em Right Seminar in Las Vegas, a city I really enjoy—great food, amazing hotels, and it's an incredible place to wander around and people-watch. I walked into one of my favorite massive casinos and looked around in wonderment at the vast numbers of people from every walk of life, vigorously playing various slot machines, roulette wheels, blackjack tables, and more.

Now in case you're not aware, casinos are notorious for having the odds stacked on the side of the House. In other words, chances are, you will lose if you play for an extended period of time. Even if you're "up," if you keep playing, the House is going to take it back because the odds just aren't on your side.

And yet all around me in this glitzy casino, I watched people playing these games, and flinging hard-earned money into these machines or down on the tables, knowing full well that they would probably lose. Some of them didn't even look like they were having any fun while doing it!

So why are they doing it? Because there is that small hope that they will hit it big—that they will walk away with more money than they could have dreamed of, while hoping they'll be smart enough to walk out of there before they lose it all back!

I started to think about SendOutCards, and how **good** our "odds" are. In SOC, we already know how much money we are laying down on the table. It's a finite amount. If we find three or four people the rest of our lives to share it with, who agree how great it is, our original outlay comes back to us 100% or higher.

If we continue to share it, even at a moderate pace, our odds of creating some kind of small monthly residual income are 100%. Even if that's only $50 a month, that's something right? Wouldn't you pick up a $50 bill if you saw it lying on the street, and tell everyone how lucky you were that day?

If we share it **actively** with others, our chances of creating an ongoing residual income, which keeps on coming and keeps on growing, are 100%. If that's $1,000 to $3,000 per month in residuals at a moderate scenario, wouldn't that pay for your mortgage payment? Car payment?

And if we give this business the weight that it deserves, and treat it not as a mere hobby, but as a business that we **dedicate our energies** to consistently by following the duplicatable system provided for us, we can generate massive residual income and financial freedom for ourselves and for our family, for life. What would you do with that $10,000 a month...$30,000 a month...$1 million a month? What could that do for you and people you care about? More importantly, do you believe you can?

And **unlike** a casino, if you build your business and do the work, your chances of achieving success just get **better and better** the longer you play. The odds are literally increasing in your favor every day.

So, let's see. Worst case scenario: You become a SOC distributor, you suddenly turn into a secret agent for no explicable reason, and decide never to tell a single soul about it. You'll make no money, but at least you've purchased an amazing tool that you can use for life to be in better touch with the people you care about. (What do the people in the casino have to show for **their** worst case scenario, besides calls from a debt collector?)

Medium scenario: You will at least make back all your money, get to use an amazing system for life for free, and generate some monthly residual income that just keeps on coming.

Best case scenario: You generate massive wealth and financial freedom, and the ability to achieve everything you've ever worked for and dreamed about.

How do those odds look?

So who wants to play?

PAINT THE PICTURE

When you share SOC with others, you must be an artist and a framer at the same time. You need to *paint the picture* of what the value is, why they need it, and what's going to happen next for them. You need to *frame it* in such a way that they feel comfortable taking those steps with you. This goes both for showing them why they need the tool, and also for painting a vision of what this business can truly do for their lives with consistent activity. Paint and frame, paint and frame...and voilà, you'll have a masterpiece!

Conveying the value of the tool to the person or group you're sharing it with is crucial. This system is incredible, but if you are not able to show them why they need it, why it is going to help them, why it is going to save them money, or why it's going to make them money, then they are not going to be prompted to do anything differently than they've always done.

That goes for many things in life. Without the need or desire, there is no action. So instill in them why this is something that really is going to make their life better, and keep the focus on them. If you don't successfully convey the value of SOC, they'll "like it" but they'll never see why they need it. And they will certainly never experience the "can't live without it" phenomenon, as so many of us do.

Next, after you share the different ways they could get started, always set them at ease by telling them what the next step will be. "After you get all set up with your account, we'll schedule a time to show you more about the system." Or, "As soon as we set up your free website, we'll set up a few three-ways calls so I can help you share it with your friends who will like it!" If they know what's going to happen next, they're not as worried to take that step outside their comfort zone. I use the analogy of, "Take their hand, tuck them in and give them warm milk." People want to feel supported and secure enough to take that next step with you. This doesn't mean you'll be doing everything for them; it just means you're going to support them in achieving whatever it is that they hope to get out of it.

Similarly for team members and prospects considering the business, you must also paint the picture for some of what your vision is for this company and your place in it; your "why," what the true possibilities are, and where you're going with it. It's not enough to just write your "I am" statements and paint a portrait for yourself. Share your painting with others. When they see your strong vision and certainty, it helps them see and believe what this can be for them as well.

ADD A TOOL TO THEIR TOOLBOX

If someone thinks you are trying to replace what they already are doing well, they are going to be defensive. If a realtor is happy with the direct-mail postcards he sends out for only 5 cents apiece, he is going to wonder, "Why would I spend a dollar per card?" He's right—he wouldn't! For that kind of a mailing, why would he?

Or if someone is extremely proud of their handwritten cards on their monogrammed stationery, it's great that they do that really well. You wouldn't dream of having them stop doing that!

SendOutCards is not meant to replace something that's already working well for them. Instead, always keep the focus on what the system will allow them to do, that they are not doing enough of currently.

So maybe the realtor sends out his direct-mail to a thousand people in a neighborhood and that brings 20 people to his open house. Now he can use SOC to send those 20 people a personalized card in his personalized handwriting with his signature, with pictures of the house they visited, saying how nice it was to meet them.

And what if those handwritten thank-you cards that she loves are out the door, but now with the addition of SOC she can also easily send out referral gifts and follow-up cards throughout the year, to continue keeping in touch with those special clients.

SOC allows you to take your relationships a step further. It is meant to round out what you maybe are **not** doing, and be another tool in your arsenal.

Maybe they are not sending birthday cards to all of their clients. Maybe they are not personalizing their holiday cards with an individual message. Maybe on a day-to-day basis, if their client mentions that his mom is in the hospital or she just got a promotion, they are not getting a card out to that person in a convenient and personal way that's geared toward that situation. Maybe they're not sending their clients appreciation gifts.

SendOutCards allows them to do all those things and more. This system is meant to supplement those things that they're already good about doing, and give them a way to do what they're not doing, to really set themselves apart from their competition. Seek to enhance, not replace, and no one can argue with you about the benefits!

ENJOY THE JOURNEY!

I'll never forget when an independent rep for a skincare company, in describing to me why she started her business, said, "I don't love selling lipstick. I didn't dream about one day schlepping eye shadow out of my trunk of my car. But that's the **vehicle** for how I can get everything I want in life."

And that explanation made sense to me at the time—that she was focusing on the big picture and working toward her "why," notwithstanding the fact that she had to do something she wasn't necessarily passionate about to get to those things. She had done a great job of "framing" why she got into her business, and I accepted that.

However, now that I'm in the MLM industry myself, I still remember those words clearly in my head, and I feel so lucky because, guess what? I do love using SOC. And I love sharing SendOutCards with others.

So doesn't that make it a lot easier to recommend it to people? Instead of saying, "Come on, just do this even though it's not fun because you'll have a great result in the long run," you're in essence saying, "Use this really amazing tool **and** get paid to share it with others!" There's nowhere in there that you're suffering and *waiting it out* just so you can become rich.

Our product is wonderfully unique, less expensive than the store, more convenient, and a lot of fun to use. We don't have to just "get through" the selling lipstick part to get to the payoff. We also get to enjoy the journey along the way.

Just through the act of sending great cards to others, people will naturally ask about them. And if someone doesn't get an account right away after you show it to them, the true value of the system will come through when you continue to keep in touch with them over time by sending great cards.

People already know that they aren't very good at reaching out to people through cards and gifts in general, so the actual arrival of your card *strengthens their recognition for why they need it*! I've even had people who have said "no" to getting set up with the system, and then they receive my card saying thank you so much anyway for your time, and they've called me back to say "You know what? I really DO need this."

Always send a thank you card when people say no. Create a campaign if you want, but always thank them for their time. Sometimes I even enjoy adding a gift. It's my version of having the "last laugh," in a heartfelt way of course! It confidently establishes, "My system is so cool that it even allows me to send you brownies when you don't want to be a part of what I have to offer. Can you do that?" It's the ultimate example of giving without expecting anything in return, and it feels **good!** And let me tell you, it makes a lasting impression.

DON'T BE THAT GUY

A guy called me the other day whom I hadn't talked to in almost two years. I'd been sending cards and gifts to both him and his wife for their birthdays and anniversary, but hadn't heard from either of them in ages. Suddenly, out of the blue, he called me and within two minutes of the conversation, started in on his sales pitch to recruit me for another network marketing company that he apparently just started and was excited about.

So I was listening to him, all the while thinking, "You haven't really earned my time here. You haven't called me in almost two years, and you immediately launched into trying to sell me something because you know I'm a 'good networker.'" Hmmm. Is that giving to *give* or giving to *get*?

Don't be the person that no one hears from unless you want something. Everyone knows a person like that. Some people **are** the "person like that" and don't know it!

SOC allows you to keep in touch with the people in your life on a regularly basis **without** wanting something from them. So if you ever do want something, it's not going to come across that way. Add value to people's lives every day, because we **can!**

SOC HAPPENS!

It was an absolutely gorgeous day in Sarasota, Florida, and I had just returned from a Treat'em Right Seminar. I'd had an incredible weekend with amazingly positive people. I had spent time laughing with old friends and bantering with new ones, and flew home with the strong reaffirmation that I absolutely love coaching and training others toward their goals.

I was contemplating how much I loved my life as I walked toward my car in the airport parking lot, and smiled as I saw my freshly washed new Infiniti shining in the sunshine, with my "SOC Star" license plate. I reached the car, humming softly, put my suitcase in the trunk, came around to the driver's side door and...Is that...wha...you're kidding me. There was bird poop EVERYWHERE. I'm talking, there was so much poop, the bird must have been the size of a pterodactyl! On the trunk, on the mirrors, on the headlights—even in the cracks of the windshield wipers! It was hilarious.

And I just stopped and started to laugh out loud, in aisle A5 of the Sarasota airport parking lot. And I think I chuckled for most of my journey home. Because yes, even when things are going well, you're going to get pooped on sometimes. In fact, it's almost guaranteed. All you can do is laugh, or at the very least learn from it, and store the lesson in your sock drawer to draw on for another day.

Yes, when negative things happen, it can be disappointing, demotivating, and even give you pause to wonder why you're doing this business in the first place. *Everyone* has those days. The one guarantee is that no one is exempt from things that inevitably go wrong and knock you off course.

But those moments often force you to revisit your "why" and strengthen your resolve that giving up or stopping isn't an option for you. Use that opportunity to take stock and gain perspective of the situation. Andrew Carnegie had a great saying: "Anything in life worth having is worth working for," so it stands to reason that we may have to refocus our efforts a bit to stay on our SOC GPS path to our destination.

DON'T BE A
SOC PUPPET

One of my least favorite questions from prospective distributors, usually spoken in a skeptical, wary tone is, "Well, how much money can you **make** at this?" Or how about when they say, "Well, I heard that so-and-so is only making such-and-such!"

What an odd thing for people to focus on. Why let what other people are doing be the determining factor for whether **you're** going to plunk down your distributor sign-up fee and get started? Shouldn't your decision rest entirely on whether you see the value in the tool, whether you can think of anyone else who would like it, and whether you believe in yourself? When you discover you'll make back all your money even if you only bring on three or four distributors the rest of your life, why would you waste your time worrying about whether you'll make millions before you even get started?

In my experience, the people who ask a million questions about the compensation plan and what the top leaders of the company are making are the ones who end up doing absolutely nothing. Yet the ones who just see the possibilities and jump in are the ones who get to the top.

You know the *Jerry Maguire* quote, "You had me at hello?" Well, when I found out about SOC, they seriously had me at the words "$120," which is what the commission was back when I first signed up—and now the commission has gone up to $140! That's a lot of money that you'll make right away, by sharing a cool tool that no one even knows about yet, **and** everyone wishes they were better at being in touch with people, **and** this is a cheaper and easier way for them to do it! Not to mention, if you keep building, the residuals and bonuses really come into play, and it just keeps getting better from there. Do the activities, and the rest will come. And it **really** will come.

Just start sharing this system with people and **GO,** instead of worrying whether this is going to work. You could have signed someone up already by the time you've finished asking the question if you can make any money in this business. It's not about what anyone else is doing or has done before you—it's what you do.

Doubting will not get you anywhere. Be that person who does it! When I saw SOC for the first time, I didn't sit around and worry how much I could make and how much other people were making. It never even crossed my mind! I immediately saw the possibilities of what I could do with this opportunity in front of me. The real issue when people ask that question is that they're looking for a reason to not even start. So believe me, they'll find a reason. They always do.

I AM JORDINA

My journey in SOC is a perfect example of how anyone can do well and start **now,** and get to the top of their dreams and goals. A few months after I started my business, I sent a card to Eagle Distributor Jordan Adler for his 50th birthday, when he was launching his first book, *Beach Money: Creating Your Dream Life Through Network Marketing.*

The front of the card had a photo of me with a voice bubble that said "Hi! I'm Jordina." I had just gotten to the rank of Senior Manager, and I wanted him to know how much I appreciated his Monday night calls and leadership. Of course, he had no idea who I was, but this is what I wrote:

Dear Jordan,

*Happy Birthday! I have been joking to my friends since I began SendOutCards that when I eventually met you I would introduce myself as "**Jordina**" because I am so passionate about the company and am working hard at building my business!*

***I have just been promoted to Senior Manager, with 27 distributors** and I recently won the Majesty of the Seas cruise, which I cannot attend unfortunately because I will be singing professionally with the New York City Ballet in London at the exact time of the cruise! Bad timing!*

*I wanted to introduce myself to you to let you know that **you have made a strong impact on me,** in your trainings, your point of view, your non-hard-sell approach, and all of your suggestions and priorities. I have always felt from the start that this business is built on relationships and interpersonal connections, and it is **reassuring to see my views consistently confirmed in your approach.***

*I look forward to meeting you and others at the Salt Lake City conference. My husband and I will be attending, and I welcome the chance to meet the other top point earners. I'm so excited to learn more from everyone, as I **have only been in the business for a couple months and can't wait to see where it will be in another year or two.***

*Thank you for the wisdom of your experience and for serving as an inspiration **to people like me way down the line! I hope to follow not too long in your footsteps.** In the meantime, I will be buying your book for my team members on your birthday, and I look forward to all that is to come!*

Warmest regards,

Jules

I highlighted certain sections of that card because I really want to point out that I was a brand new distributor in March of 2008 with 27 distributors, when Jordan had no idea who I was, and mine was just one of hundreds of birthday cards he received. But I believed with all my being that I was going to be at the top of this wonderful company, along with the people I'd admired from afar.

One of the first times that I spoke to Kathy Paauw, a top 10 income-earner and Executive Distributor in my upline, she told me about something called "The Eagle's Nest," which was comprised of the top 10 income-earners and the top 10 point-earners in the challenges over a six-month period. I loved the idea that someone who was relatively new like me could be on a weekly call with our CEO and founder and have a voice in what was going on. I made up my mind that I would qualify for the very next one.

Sure enough, six months later, I ended up as #2 in the points challenge out of the entire company and attended my first SOC convention as an Eagle's Nest member. I began to meet and form relationships with the people whose names I'd only read about. I continued to move forward in my business consistently, and even as a Senior Manager, I moved up into the Top 20 in income. By my second SOC convention, I had been promoted to Executive.

My "I am" was so strong—"I am Jordina." From day one, I never doubted that I was in the right place at the right time, and that this company was in line with all that I am and believe in.

The reason I mention all this is to make this extremely important point: **Anyone** with a passion, a drive, belief, and hard work can be successful in SOC. In fact, people who know a lot more about network marketing than I do have told me that the biggest leaders in this business haven't even come in to the company yet! Maybe that person is you.

Isn't it exciting to know you can catch up, or even *surpass* what anyone has managed to do so far? How inspiring is that? This isn't one of those companies where the leaders are making a "kachillion" dollars, and they're legends among the masses who have no chance of reaching that level. In SOC, the leaders are you and me. Anyone can start today and just do it.

SOCS-PECTATIONS

"Don't feel entitled to anything you don't sweat and struggle for."

Marian Wright Edelman, American activist,
founder of the Children's Defense Fund

You're not entitled to have other people working the business under you. If people sign up and do nothing, that's their prerogative. In the beginning, I always say, pretend you have a job that pays you $140 to $315 in 30 minutes and pretend that the extra bonuses and residual income that follow are a happy surprise when they do start to accumulate.

Yes, the network marketing model is based on the fact that you will get paid on the efforts of lots of other people as you continue to build. But if you are going to be successful in this business, you can't allow yourself to get disappointed by what people are not doing, or feel cheated if they're not doing what they say they will.

I remember so clearly one day when a distributor in my downline called me up, and almost in tears said, "I've signed up 13 people, and no one's doing *anything!*" She was actually feeling betrayed. There was a little silence, and I quietly said, "Yeah. And?"

Network marketing is a gift, not an entitlement. Meaning, when the model does start to work for you, and the time leveraging starts to take its magic shift, and the bike comes down the other side of the hill without you peddling, that's the magic and that's the gift that this industry allows us to experience.

But to be angry that "no one's doing anything?" Try to manage those expectations before they eat you up. There are people in this business who signed up 100 people before anyone on their team started "doing anything." And there are people whose very first distributor they signed up started working the business.

The one thing you can be sure of? People will rarely do what they **say** they're going to do, or what you **think** they're going to do. The more you focus on what you can control, the better.

If you move on and just sign people up, keep in constant activity, and help the people who want to be helped, people will eventually follow your lead, and you **will** reap the benefits of being in a network marketing business. But just keep going. Why would they want to join your movement if you're not moving!

You know the famous line from *Field of Dreams*, "If you build it, they will come?" They will. But that starts with the "building it" part. I don't remember anywhere Kevin Costner saying, "If you sit around and stare at them, or turn around and yell at them, they will eventually do something."

If you get easily discouraged by the fact that no one is doing anything, and you let that frustrate you or make you feel betrayed, you will most likely miss out on the long-term benefits that come with having patience in this industry. Be the example to your team. Even if no one else does anything, you **still** get well-paid for your **own** time and efforts in this business. But your chances of things getting even better will increase if you don't give up.

Plus, you will automatically attract the right people into your business when you *become* the person that you want on your team. You being "your best you" will bring out the best in others! Stop expecting something from others, and expect it from yourself. *You* are in control of your success—no one else.

JUST SEND IT!

Christine Eisenman of Clearwater, Florida, was a brand new SOC distributor in 2007 and had only personally sponsored two distributors into her new SendOutCards business. One day, she sent a birthday card to a woman she had never met, whom she'd only spoken to her on the phone once about possibly joining her women's group. While creating the card, she got to the gift section, attached a $5 Starbucks gift card, and pressed "send."

There was probably a moment in there where she thought, "Ah, I won't send a gift. I don't even know her, and I'll probably never even hear if she got this card." We've all experienced that moment. But Christine did it anyway and sent it off, with a give-to-give mentality.

So who was the lucky recipient of the unexpected heartfelt birthday card? Me! I got two cards in my mailbox on my birthday that year: one from my mom and one from Christine.

I opened up this card from a girl I'd never met. I read the simple note in her card, and looked in amazement at the $5 Starbucks card. I was totally blown away—a girl I'd never met sent me a birthday card and a Starbucks card? I found her email with her phone number in it, and I called her to thank her for the card and the gift. I was truly surprised and touched.

She said, "Oh, I'm so glad you liked it! I have a tool that allows me to do things like that, to remember birthdays and to send things to people I care about and even people I don't know very well. If you're at your computer I can show you how it works."

Well, I was. And she did. And the rest is history. I have been a SOC-a-hol-ic and in-SOC-niac for almost three years now and have sent over 8,000 cards and gifts to the people I care about. And Christine? She's pretty happy about it too.

So yes, I was the third distributor that Christine signed up, and proceeded to build a large team, so she never had to say, "My distributors aren't doing *anything!*" In fact, she got to experience what many people are still waiting to see for their own eyes—that this business "works!" (Even though there's nothing to "work" as we discussed earlier!)

But so what if it takes you until your 100th distributor or your 500th distributor for your team to take off running...what possible reason would you ever have to stop? You'll certainly never get there if you don't continue to share it with others. Would you really rather stop trying just because it's not coming quickly enough? What kind of logic is that?

Now let's get back to that Starbucks card for a moment. We all like to think that we give to give, but do you really and truly? If you ever have those little pauses where you think "No, I won't send this because I won't get anything back for it," **do it anyway!** Send it and forget it. Don't place expectations on what you'll possibly receive in return. What if Christine had? I would not be here today and you would definitely not be reading this book!

I can honestly say that for me, it was the addition of that gift card—the selfless act of that little gift card perched inside my simple, heartfelt birthday card—that blew me away and made me call Christine to say "Wow, why did you do that? And **how?**"

The act of sending that $5 Starbucks gift card to a girl she'd never met has vastly changed her life and her family's life, just as it's forever changed mine. And don't forget that the impact keeps on going, because the 1,000 people in my downline (and the thousands still to come) are all changed because of that $5 Starbucks card as well. Now that's some strong coffee!

SOC HOP

In the Treat'em Right Seminars, SendOutCards Founder and CEO Kody Bateman speaks about what it means to be a "Level Four Card Sender," meaning you don't have to think about it. You just do it. Well, most of you are "Level Four sock-wearers." You put socks on every day, right? (Well unless you live in Florida like me, but for the most part you don't think about it before you put on your socks and then your shoes.)

It started out as something your mom had to remind you to do when you were little, and now you just do it. It's a habit. It would feel awfully strange to put on your shoes without socks first.

Yet one of the biggest surprises for me when I started my business is that people don't take any initiative to make the crucial, result-producing activities of this business into a habit. They have the ability to make money every single day, yet they don't work it into their lives because they "get busy." How can it slip to last priority so quickly?

If I called someone up right now and said, "I'll give you $300 today if you help me pick out my outfit this morning," how many people would get themselves to my house and make that happen? Most people would show up on my doorstep if they possibly could, right? So with SOC, are they just *forgetting* that they have a chance to make great income every day by sharing this tool and business with others?

I sometimes like to throw out fun challenges with my team like "Windfall Wednesday!" or "Moneybags Monday," offering small token prizes, for anyone who signs up a distributor that day, or for doing a certain number of walkthroughs in a month, etc. I do this partly to make things even more fun for my team, but partly to remind them that it exists!

And every time, it always surprises me how people will come out of the woodwork, having done nothing for months, just to "win" the reward. Why should it take that extra one-time prize to spur people into action, when they have the ability to make those coaching bonuses every single day—not to mention all the residuals that consistent activity will bring?

So if that sounds like you, if you hop into instant action at the promise of a prize you suddenly want to win, then do yourself a favor and pretend that SendOutCards calls you up every morning:

(RING, RING!)

You: Hello?

SOC: Hi! It's SendOutCards.

You: Hey! How are ya?

SOC: Great! I just called to let you know that today, I'm offering you $$$$$ for everyone that you bring into your team today.

You: Really? That's awesome!

SOC: I know!

You: So all I have to do is call someone, show them how **they** can send great cards this way, and even make extra income, and you will pay me $$$$?

SOC: Yep! And even more than that, we'll pay you residuals on every card that person ever sends. So your hard work is actually building **toward** something.

You: Wow, now that's awesome. I can definitely find time to do that. It only takes about 30 minutes right?

SOC: Yes, that's right. And it will help someone else be in better touch with the people they care about.

You: That's so amazing. Thank you so much for the offer. I feel so lucky to have this chance!

SOC: No problem! I will be calling you again tomorrow!

Find your own drive to do this for yourself, every day, and know that you're building toward something a lot more amazing than even those great coaching bonuses. You're building toward a lifetime of residuals that will change your entire future.

"It's easy to stay active. It's also easy not to. And if you stop, it won't kill you today—but that simple error in judgment, compounded over time, will absolutely destroy that getting of any goal you're after."
Jeff Olson, *The Slight Edge*

It's so simple but so true! The little things in life are easy to do, and easy not to do. It is so hard to make yourself do those small tasks, when it seems like there isn't a penalty for letting it go one more day.

Yes, eating that *one* piece of cake won't make you fat. But consistently choosing the wrong decisions will move you in the wrong direction pretty fast. Even the little things accumulate over time, and you are always either traveling in a positive or negative direction, toward or away from your goals.

Jordan Adler once said about this opportunity of financial freedom: "It is possible, it is happening, and it can happen for you." It absolutely can! But hoping it will isn't enough. You have to do the **consistent activities** that will move you toward your desired result.

I love this quote from Carrie Fisher: "There is no point at which you can say, "Well, I'm successful now. I might as well take a nap."

Why would anyone ever stop? Is it difficult or hard to keep mentioning something that people like, when you'll get paid to share it?

If I were to tell you that you are **guaranteed** to make a certain amount of money if you consistently committed to doing gift account walkthroughs and follow-ups for two years straight, would you do it? Most people would if they had that guarantee, because they'd know that if they just put in their time, they will get what's due. People work a whole lifetime just to get their tiny social security or pension when they retire.

So let's say you knew you were definitely going to make $10,000 to 15,000 a month after two to three years if you did the right activities. Well, most people would probably do walk-throughs and follow-ups every single day to get there, don't you think? So why don't they? Because it's **not** guaranteed. And no, I'm not going to give you a guarantee either—sorry!

But what I can guarantee is that sending heartfelt cards and sharing the tool every day worked for me. No one had to give me a guarantee for me to see that if I did the work, the results would be wonderful. Without any regard to "how much can I make?" or "will this work?" I just started doing those activities with no excuses from day one. And does it "work?" Absolutely!

As Thomas Huxley says, "Do what you should do, when you should do it, whether you feel like it or not." Don't you want to be making the right choices, even if you can't see the result right away? Do the activities and trust that the rest will follow. So, what are you waiting for? Turn the dial up to Level Four and hop to it!

BE UNSHAKEABLE

So if you're consistently sharing SOC with others, I imagine you've received a few objections here and there. One of my favorite ones is "Oh, I like to *hand-write* cards." With that little superior tone and a slight sneer as they look down their nose at you—you know what I'm talking about, right?

And I've actually heard distributors say in response to that, "Oh yes, I know, it's the best to get a handwritten card, but with SOC it allows you to send it more easily and faster, and it really saves you time and allows you to send more than you would have normally."

What? You'd seriously rather get a card on some boring stationary with a monogram in scrawling pen that you can barely read that says a few niceties? No way! Don't apologize or imply that SOC isn't as good as a card in a store. I don't use SendOut-

Cards because it's faster (**and** easier **and** less expensive)—even though it is all of those things. If I had **all day** to send a card to someone, with no other tasks to accomplish, I would **still** send a SendOutCard.

It's not an "almost-as-good, second-hand substitute!" It's way more personal than a store card, with those photos and captions and thought bubbles. There is a reason why people say "that's the best card I've ever gotten," and why they display these cards on their desks and refrigerators.

You can bet that in about 2.7 seconds after someone reads that lovely monogrammed stationery card with beautiful matching color-trimmed envelope, and thinks, "Huh, that's nice," you'll hear "Whoosh!" (That was the sound of it fluttering into the trash can.)

Yet a SendOutCard gets saved and displayed and passed around, and it brings back memories, elicits laughter, and touches people. The photographs are priceless, and the immediacy of being able to respond to something—even a small thing—makes the cards timely and powerful.

Oh, and by the way, it's certainly possible to send a boring SendOutCard—but DON'T. Take an extra second to personalize it and that recipient will remember it forever.

Yes, you will hear objections. Meet them head-on with confidence and without apology. If they don't see it the way you see it, that's okay, but there are thousands and thousands of card senders who are on **your** side. Just go find more.

RUNNING SOCS

At a Treat'em Right Seminar in Atlanta last year, Jordan Adler called up a few leaders in the front of the room and asked us to answer a few questions: How long we've been in SOC, how many distributors we have, and how many distributors make up the largest percentage of overall volume in our business (or how many "legs" we have.) I was excited to be included in such an esteemed bunch, despite the fact that I had been in SOC for a shorter amount of time than they had, and I had a much smaller number of distributors than they did.

I listened to each leader's answers as Jordan we went down the line, and they each said "Two legs." "Three legs." "Two legs." "Three legs." And it was getting closer and closer to my turn to answer.

As I heard them all talking about their two or three "legs" of income, I started thinking about how I still hadn't "found anyone like me yet," so when it was my turn, I answered jokingly, "I'm still looking for my legs!" Well, of course everyone laughed, and the rest of the weekend it was a cute joke of people yelling out "I'll be your leg," etc.

But later on, I started to think about a couple things. What if you don't have legs to put your socks on? Here I was, a top 20 income-earner in the company, with no big "legs" to speak of! Although of course I wanted some big ol' legs, how exciting that you can have a very successful business, even with a lot of people doing a little bit.

But later I realized that in actuality, I have about ten legs. Although no one leg stands out hugely above another, there is a pretty even volume spread across the board with about ten active distributors before it tapers way off. As my team continues to grow, this will probably shift more toward the two or three legs that most leaders do tend to have, with a very large proportion of distributors who "do nothing."

Jordan's point, of course, is that no matter the size of your organization, you're looking for those aces. Even if you have 10,000 or 60,000 distributors, you'll probably have most of your volume coming from the downline of two or three people who really take it and run with it.

But the great thing is, if you really train people to use the tools and resources that are in place, as well as paint the picture for them of the culture and inspire their vision, who's to say you won't have a veritable millipede of decent legs...Just think of all the socks they'll need!

DON'T DIP
YOUR PINKY TOE

In my opinion, the single most important event you can go to that will take your business to the next level is the SendOut-Cards Annual Convention. Have you committed to going to the next one? So many people say, "Next year, next year." It isn't a luxury. The leaders get themselves there. Period. Immerse yourself in this business and the rest will follow.

Are you waiting until you become successful in SOC to go to those events? How do you think you're going to become success-ful? If you started a conventional business, wouldn't you be sure you had all the training you needed to make your venture suc-cessful, even if you had to invest your money toward the licens-ing, courses, mentors and materials to ensure your success?

I've seen brand new reps with very demanding jobs who turned around and booked tickets to the convention about a week after they signed up! And I've seen people who think they're working the business but have never even considered making the effort to go, and they wonder why things aren't going faster for them.

Successful people get themselves there. Wouldn't you be surprised if you ever heard a top leader say, "Nawwww—I'm not going to go to the convention this year. I already know all that stuff!"? Again, successful people get themselves there; no excuses. And if all the successful people do it, don't you want to be one of them? Simply hoping this will work is not going to build you a successful business.

Put in the effort; don't put in your pinky toe!

SOC-IGNITION

Give recognition to your team. Find ways to celebrate their achievements, even if they're small. Order name tags for them when they get a promotion. Organize small team get-togethers. Have little challenges. Give out little presents to reward the right activities. Send out emails that recognize sign-ups or promotions.

They say you have to be duplicatable and that's true, but there's nothing wrong with being a leader. If you're walking the walk, they have something to aspire to. Once they've reached a certain level in their business, encourage them to do the same for their teams.

You'll see duplication at its best, because they will have learned what inspired and encouraged them. If you do special things, people will want to be a part of it. It's supposed to be fun, remember? These kinds of group gatherings inspire excitement, healthy competition and focus.

I've had Senior Managers say to me, "But I don't have a team yet! No one is working the business." My feeling is, you're a leader before you even have a single distributor, and you have a team the moment you have one member. Don't wait until you magically find five people who want to work the business to step into a leadership role! Be a leader and it will give people something to follow.

Early on in my business, I created a group called "The Knights of the SOC Table." In fact, the qualification for someone in my downline to become a Knight was that you had to have six distributors or more, because I don't think I even had any Managers in my downline yet!

I set the dates for the monthly meetings, planned a brief training, and set the tradition in motion. Everyone who qualified received a card with an invitation to join. If they were an out-of-town Knight, they got the handouts and the recaps of the meetings. I didn't wait until I had a bunch of Managers to put something in place.

Today I have over 45 Knights in the group from all over the country, but I still remember that first meeting when I only had a few and I wasn't even sure if they'd want to show up! There are brand new distributors on my team who make it their first goal to get into the Knights as soon as they hear about its existence. It feels so amazing to hear someone say "Only two more distributors and I'll be a Knight!" and knowing that I've created something of which they're proud to be a part.

There are many things you can do to lead your team. Have a monthly conference call. Send a newsletter. Gather at a coffee shop or café once a week with your laptops to brainstorm. It's that "If you build it, they will come," concept again. Instead of chasing people all over town and trying to *make* them do something, put some good systems in place, and let people tap into them when they are ready. That's SOC-nificantly better.

SOC-GANIZATION

How jumbled and messy is your drawer? Get organized. The best thing you can do for yourself is to have a good system for yourself that works. Not only will it keep you organized, but again it gives your team something to duplicate.

I like to use a simple binder system that has plastic business card sleeves and tabs for the 31 days of the month. In it, I place the business cards of my prospects on the day I'm supposed to call them. These people are the lucky recipients of my magic sentence over and over again as I consistently "move them through" the book!

I label my dividers Monday 1, Tuesday 1, Wednesday 1, Thursday 1, Friday 1, etc., and then I do the same with Monday 2, 3, 4, and 5 and so on. These dividers correspond to the first

Monday of the month, the second Monday of the month, etc. Or, you could also get 31 dividers and simply label them 1 to 31, to correspond to all the days in the month if you prefer. The last divider is labeled "Contact in the Future."

Every time I meet a new prospect, I send them a greeting card and then put their business card into the book to follow up five days later. I also keep some blank perforated business cards on my desk, so that every time someone mentions they'd be interested in looking at the system, or if someone gives me a referral, I grab a blank card and write down all the info I have for them to put it in the follow-up binder.

My goal is simply to move the cards through the book. I personally like this process rather than a computerized system, because every day you can open your book and see who you need to call. If you call someone on a Monday, let's say, and they're not there, you can make a decision when you want to call again, and move them to Thursday. If you call someone who was supposed to be there but didn't answer, you can move that card to the following day. If they tell you that they need until next Monday to decide, move it from Monday 1 to Monday 2. In other words, you can always decide on the spot when you'd like to call them again, and move the card to the proper day.

If you don't get to all the calls you need to make for that day, simply take the pages out and move them to the next day! No harm done. There are no card emergencies, and we can only do what we can.

Even after someone gets an account, you can leave their name in the book for a while, moving it through to remind yourself to check in on them and see if they have questions and how they're doing with the system. The most important thing is to always write down anyone who may be interested when that situation arises, so you always remember to follow up at some point and no one falls through the cracks.

There are many, many ways you can get organized, and this is just one I like that has worked well for me. The most important thing to do is find a system that works for you and stick to it. If you're not organized now, it will be hard to move forward and stay on top of everything as your team grows and grows.

Your organization is the cornerstone of your business. Many people in SendOutCards have never had to deal with sales, follow-up, training, personalities, phone calls and emails before. They get into this business because they love the tool and the opportunity, and then they find themselves suddenly struggling with the skills they wish they'd paid more attention to in school.

If this sounds like you, it's all right. It doesn't have to overwhelm you as long as you're aware that you need to improve in this area. Try various things, find what works for you, and then stick to it consistently—and keep your drawer a jumble-free zone!

DIRTY SOCS

Kody Bateman talks in his Treat'em Right Seminar about dropping the "old tennis balls" that don't serve you anymore in life. It is crucial to do that to move forward in your business. Similarly, you must periodically clean out your SOC Drawer. There is nothing wrong with having an overflowing drawer, as long as every sock still has a purpose and a positive message to share.

But if you're holding onto anything in your sock drawer that's old and "grimy," as Kody says, then it's time to evaluate it, toss it and replace it with a pair that fits your more current circumstance and still serves your current goals and direction.

Just washing or patching up your socks isn't going to do it. When they've run their course, face it—it's time for them to go!

SOC-SISTENCY

Although you want to keep your drawer free from dirty socks, you also don't want to change your socks every five minutes. Be consistent with your message to your team. If people get confused, they'll do nothing. Don't say, "Okay guys, now do this!"

Have you noticed that Jordan Adler never changes his message over the years? He doesn't create new tools that come and go, or tell everyone to go send out a new campaign card or gift that he designed for a particular occasion. He doesn't tell people to take out ads in the newspaper or buy leads or do trade shows.

Jordan always says the same thing. *Send heartfelt cards and share the system and opportunity with others.* There are new tools coming out all the time, but keep your message to your team simple and consistent, and let them use whatever other tools or methods they choose that appeal to them individually.

Another way that people change their socks too often is to jump from business opportunity to business opportunity. There was a distributor on my team, down on my fifth level or so, who absolutely loved SOC and really saw the true value in a deep and significant way. He wrote me this email one day, which I saved because it really touched me:

Jules,

I continue to immerse myself in SOC. I learn something every time I log in. I talked to four different people on the phone yesterday. Each of them agreed to meet me the week after next. I am not kidding, I think SOC is something so special, so different, at such a perfect time, I just cannot wait to tell people about it. I have not felt this energy in a long time. SOC has given me permission to reach out to people I had lost contact with. The best part is...almost everyone I talk to feels the same way.

Thanks for your patience, understanding and leadership! I look forward to tapping into your knowledge for a long, long time!

Sincerely, xxxxx

And yet shortly after writing that email, he somehow let his fears and doubts and excuses and "life getting busy" all creep in, and the next thing I heard, he had jumped into some other opportunity because SOC "didn't work for him." What? Do you think this other business will work for him, most likely? Or does the problem lie somewhere else? He is letting his fears of success and failure get in the way of the clear passion and vision that he had!

Now, it's not my job to call and scold and convince, but I just feel sad for him, all those lost opportunities. What is it that makes someone go from writing those beautiful words to telling himself that something isn't for them?

It reminds me of a time in New York City when I was dating a guy for three months...let's just call him Pete (mostly because that's his name). Everything was going great and we always had the best time together—not a ripple in the waters.

And one night after a romantic "Three Month-A-Versary" dinner, (completely **his** idea!) to celebrate our third month of dating, I headed home to prepare for an audition early the next morning. When I got home, I already had a message on my voicemail from him that went on and on and on about how I was the best thing that had ever happened to him, and he couldn't believe I had come into his life...blah, blah, you get the idea. Very sweet.

The next morning, I woke up and started getting ready for my audition, when the phone rang. It was Pete, who then proceeded to break up with me. I kid you not! No reason, no explanation, and no mention of him having professed how I'm the best thing that's ever happened to him the night before. Just an odd, robotic-sounding Pete, saying that it wasn't going to work out. (I actually saved that message for ages to play for people just to prove that I wasn't crazy!)

As a side note (because this truly would have made a good sit-com), my audition that morning was for a Gershwin musical, so after I finished getting "broken up with" over the phone, I ironically had to head immediately to midtown in time to sing the Gershwin song, "Our Love Is Here to Stay," which I had prepared for that day. Yeah, good times. You can't make this stuff up.

But do you see the similarity? In both cases, that crazy human tendency crept in, when they connected to something deeply, and then all of a sudden, what sets in? **Fear.** Your brain starts racing ahead and working out various scenarios and telling you all the reasons why something's **not** going to work before you've even begun to give it a chance. I call this The Hump. You either make it over the hump, or you hit that wall and go racing backwards.

In dating, when people hit the hump of fear, they make a clean break with their current situation, and run off to start all over again with someone new, because it's easier than dealing with their feelings. In network marketing when they hit the hump, people abandon what they clearly saw the value of before, and they go seek something else shinier, believing that this time it will work for them.

And as a bystander to this, all you can truly do is shake your head and **let them go.** In both cases, they'll eventually realize that the problem lies with them—not the company and **definitely** not the girlfriend...for Pete's sake!

JOY OF SOCS

Are you a joy to be around? Or do people screen you when you call? Strive to always be the kind of person who will cause someone to look down and smile when they see your name flash on their screen. That's when you know that you've done your job of adding value to others.

If you're brave enough to test it out, when you spot a friend on the street, call them on their cell while you're watching them from afar and see what they do. But be prepared—it's not pretty to see them pull it out, shake their head, and stuff it back into their bag!

Use the cards and gifts to strengthen your relationships with people. Look for ways to help others. Give to give, not get. Help and encourage your team members far beyond what you get "paid to do." Always support and edify your upline and crosslines when you have the opportunity. Express appreciation to others whenever possible.

Take an interest in people, whether or not you feel they can "benefit" you in some way. Try to complain as little as possible. Smile a lot! Let your actions speak louder than words. Remind yourself often of what's positive in your life and what you have accomplished thus far, instead of always thinking about what you are still seeking or lacking.

All of these factors play a huge role in the success of both your business and personal life! Ask yourself, "Would you want to be friends with you?"

MISSING SOCS

Is it not one of the greatest universal mysteries of life that so many socks disappear in the wash? Where do they *go?* Isn't it almost impossible to understand?

Similarly, one of the greatest mysteries in SOC is how people would see the value in it, put down their hard-earned money to be a distributor...and then vanish without a trace. They tell you all the reasons that they can't wait to get started in the business, and then you can't get them on the phone, they refuse to do a three-way call, and then you find out the horrifying news that they're not even using the system to send cards!

Or, they throw themselves in, get all the way to Senior Manager, and then **stop!** What? This is when it starts to get really good! And you're *done?*

Distributors ask me all the time, "What can I do about that? What am I doing wrong?"

Well, what do you do when one of your socks goes missing? Do you cry over it? Do you decide to never wear socks again? Do you curse the sock? Do you call the other sock and demand to know where the missing one has gone? Do you whine, "I had really high hopes for that sock!" Or do you simply work with the socks you have, and go out and get another pair of socks to replace the one that's long gone?

Our SOCs are no different. Unfortunately, they disappear sometimes. The worst part for us is not knowing why or understanding how they can let such an opportunity just drop, when they've already paid the money, and they definitely saw the value. All they have to do is open their mouths and tell someone about it.

But our SOCs will go missing. And it is not our job to lament or ask why. We simply work with the socks we have, and we continually shop for more to keep our drawer filled to the brim— with the good ones.

Oh, and one final universal law of missing SOCs...sometimes they come back. And if they do, welcome them back into the drawer like old friends as if they were never gone. Because that's another great thing about SOC—it's never too late to start.

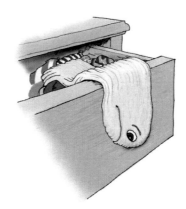

DROOPY SOCS

There is an expression in SendOutCards about finding out who you are and giving yourself away. This is so important because there are many people who haven't yet grasped the idea of sending out to give, and when they do, it truly opens up a whole new world to them.

But there are a few people who, believe it or not, actually have the opposite problem. This is rarely discussed or addressed, but I think it's important to mention.

Yes, definitely be a giver, and yes, give yourself away—but not away and away and away and away. So before I go on, we're going to do a bit of a sorting process right now. If you DON'T consider yourself a nurturer, skip to the next section gracefully. You will get a little uncomfortable during this part, and won't like it much.

Yes, of course, as in any "people-business," we have to learn how to deal with many different personality profiles. But for now, I'm only talking to a certain segment of loving, helpful do-gooders.

So all of you non-nurturers are gone now right?

Okay. Welcome all you Nurturers! How are you today? Good? Great! Okay, now we're going to go a bit further in the sorting process.

If you're a nurturer who likes to help people and be thoughtful and do nice little things, but you still manage to keeping it all in balance, then you too can skip to the next section. Yep, go ahead. Scoot.

You're still here? I mean it—this is going to get a little intense and you don't need to hear this. Okay, are you guys really gone now? Great.

So now I'm only talking to the super **uber** ridiculous, over the top, above-and-beyond'er kind of nurturer who only feels good when you're doing massive things for other people all the time. **You know who you are**. What I'm about to say is really important.

SOC attracts a lot of kind, understanding, giving, loving wonderful people; but if you're prone to giving too much, don't deplete yourself! No one wants a limp rag in their sock drawer.

There's a difference between giving yourself away and doing too much. We train our distributors on the concept of giving to give, not giving to get, but there are some of you with the opposite problem, and you are the ones still reading this. (Unless of course you cheated! But if you did, you might as well read on, because you may be able to help someone in your downline with this concept down the road!)

Those people are truly giving to give, and not intending to get something back for it, but then they give and give and give and give and one day they wake up and get depressed. Why? They don't feel appreciated. They don't feel like they are getting even a scrap back from others. They feel like all their efforts have been wasted. They feel that they've sacrificed for nothing. They feel resentful.

STOP IT!

I'm speaking from experience because I have been known to do this without meaning to do it, of course. I love to help others. I love to give freely. I love to help without strings, without boundaries, without reciprocation. And then suddenly I have those days where I have nothing left to give and I feel completely deflated. And I don't want to give anything to anyone. I'm spent.

If you've been to a Treat'em Right Seminar, you'll hear the massive amount of low self-esteem that permeates the room throughout some of the personal development exercises. It is shocking how people often devalue themselves, and how they've been taught somewhere down the road in life to put themselves last.

Giving to give is so rewarding, and when you do that in balance and harmony, it is the absolute best part of this business, and of life, for that matter. But if you go to the extreme, and it compounds on itself, then you'll actually be unintentionally expecting something in return from people, and thus you become a covert "give-to-getter." Beware!

You can be helpful, be courteous, be friendly, be an example, get people started, be accessible, be a leader, and by all means go above and beyond sometimes. But the minute you feel drained, or even resentful, you are doing too much and *expecting* too much, and the only person you have to blame for that is yourself.

So I'd like to add an addendum to the SOC tagline of "give yourself away." It really should be "give yourself away...mostly." Enough said!

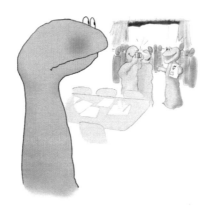

THE PANG
WITH NO NAME

What is the "The pang with no name?" Well, it's hard to describe. It's that little feeling that sneaks in when you don't get the recognition you think you deserve; when something's not fair; when you feel jealous of someone; when you wish you had something they have; when you feel they don't deserve what they have; when you see someone doing something you don't agree with; when you feel like you should be further, faster, bigger; when you hear about something you missed out on; when you don't get what you expected; when someone disappoints you.

This is such a funny business when you stop to think about it, because the entire culture of SOC is to help each other, across all team lines, in any way we can—which is what makes us great! And yet, it's a business where we compete for recognition, for top income, top ranking points, winning trips, for distributors of the year, Eagle's Nest standings and more. I know of no other business model where they encourage you to help each other so much, and at the same time recognize and rank who is doing the best at everything.

I was met with this head-on when a distributor who wasn't in my downline once called me for advice and he wanted me to help him with some things he felt like I was doing well, and he actually said to me, "If you help me, I promise I'll be gentle when I whiz past you." Does that seem odd to you, or is it just me? I was mildly annoyed, I admit.

Well, even though he was kidding (sort of), it definitely brought this strange dichotomy to light. As a competitive person in general, I wasn't sure how to deal with this. Of course I want to help everyone. And of course I want to be the best at everything. Confusing? Yeah, hence, sometimes that pang with no name creeps in.

This may surprise the people who know me, but in general, I'd say that I'm a "glass half empty" gal. Most people would have no idea. People say "You're the happiest person I've ever met, you smile all the time." Yes, I am happy and I do smile a lot, and it's genuine, definitely. But my natural tendency since I was born is to be a pessimist: To see all the reasons why something won't work! To come up with all the contingency plans.

See, I didn't consider it pessimistic per se; I always saw it as being logical and practical and reasonable! But maybe on some level, I was such a perfectionist that I also just wanted to prepare myself for any possible disappointment.

And when something goes wrong, my first instinct isn't necessarily to deal with it as well I should. I was a psychology major in college, and one of the books that had a huge impact on me was *Learned Optimism* by Martin Seligman, who had studied the behaviors and thought patterns of optimists and pessimists for 25 years. He taught the concept that changing your mind can change your life.

Dr. Seligman found that the difference between people who give up versus people who never quit is what he referred to as their "explanatory style." When good or bad events occur, our explanatory style is the way we explain or interpret those events in our minds.

A pessimist will immediately believe that bad events were somehow caused by them and will last for a while, and it stops them in their tracks. Optimists, on the other hand, believe that these negative events are just a temporary setback, usually caused by someone else! So they're able to recover faster and act again sooner, due to the way they interpret that same failure.

Two different kinds of people can face the exact same plateaus and challenges, but explain the cause differently to themselves! Let's say someone gets a promotion. The explanatory style of the optimist will cause him or her to think, "I got this promotion because I'm really good at what I do!" The explanatory style of a pessimist to the same event will cause him or her to think, "I got the promotion because I lucked out somehow, and now I'm in trouble because they'll probably be watching my actions more than ever to see if I fail." These thoughts appear instantly in your mind to "explain" away a situation. Once you're aware of it, you can really start to catch yourself in any negative patterns.

I had never thought about any of those concepts, and it was fascinating to me. I started to realize how often I tended to immediately interpret a situation in a negative way, when I could just as easily have chosen to look at it from a completely different, more empowering point of view. I still have to work at it. But I really like knowing that even if you're naturally one way, you can work on it to become better at those things overall.

So, perhaps give some thought to the qualities you embody that maybe aren't the most flattering or productive, and do a little work on it. And when people start to compliment you on the things that you always struggled with, you'll see how rewarding it can be to have made those strides.

When the pang with no name flares up, face it, deal with it, learn from it, and make the choice to grow. If it doesn't come naturally, practice until you get good. If it does come naturally, practice anyway! It's a process. It's all part of your personal development journey that goes hand-in-hand with this business. And people can change for the better.

PUT A SOC IN IT!

There are a few things you'd do well to avoid saying when introducing SOC to prospects:

You'll LOVE this!
You'd be awesome at this!
You know so many people!

Isn't that funny? All of these things seem encouraging and positive from your end, yet they're thinking:

How do you know what I'd like? I'm determined to hate it now.
Oh no, I have to "do" something and I'll never meet their expectations. Better not start.
You're just using me for my contacts.

I like to use the phrase, "I have something to show you that you might find interesting." This is a much less threatening way of getting them to the walkthrough, without telling them how they're going to feel about it.

And back to the magic sentence concepts we talked about earlier: Try to avoid energetically stringing together sentences connected with "And you can...And you can...And you can..." while attempting to describe all the neat features of SOC. At Treat'em Right Seminars, some trainers often demonstrate a funny skit of this behavior, where they act out the scenario of two people meeting at a networking event. One of them practically backs the other off the stage while proceeding to "throw up" juicy factoids all over him or her.

If people tend to run from you when they see you coming, this is your first clue that you may not have mastered this skill quite yet! Use DeMarr Zimmerman's Fast Start phrase, "It's 90% visual." And then show them more about it—don't tell them. Avoid plunging into the Valley of Death. Shhhhhh....put a sock in it!

LISTEN TO LIFE WITH SENDOUTCARDS EARS

One of the neatest things about having SendOutCards in your life is that it allows you to develop an additional level of awareness. I call it "listening to life with SendOutCards ears."

People in general let things slip by daily because they've trained their minds that they don't have time to address these things as they arise. SOC opens up an entirely new level of communication by allowing you to act every day on the things that happen around you.

I like to think of it as your seventh sense. SOC gives you the ability to lift the blinders, so you can do a little more, be a little more, and give a little more than those who don't have a system in place to take in anything more.

Be that person who does, and it will change your life and those around you. When something would make a great card, I call it "SOC-able!" Your life will be enriched if you listen and respond to these things, because we have a convenient and inexpensive mechanism to do that now.

Take a genuine interest in those you meet. Look for reasons to send appreciation, use humor, support others, and be a connector of people. Something happens every single day that you could be responding to either in kindness or humor or gratitude.

Sometimes this may lead to business or a distributor, and other times it may not, but you will be establishing yourself as a good businessperson who cares about others, and people will respect what you do. Plus, it reminds you every day why this is an incredible tool that everyone should have. Use your magical ears, and inspire others to do it too!

You have the ability to make the world a better place in 30 seconds. Instill this concept in your team members as well, both through your words and through leading by example. You'll be creating an entire culture of like-minded people who care about making a difference in the world around them.

SOC-SCUSES

"I'm so busy." Really? That's funny, I was just sitting around on my couch doing absolutely nothing when SOC fell into my lap. NOT!

Successful people aren't sitting stagnant, waiting for something to come along. They're **already** busy with a million things. But they see the opportunity and take it on and fit it in and run with it, despite the other things on their plate. I don't know a single successful person in SOC who had absolutely nothing to do when this opportunity hit their radar screen.

So many times, distributors have even told me their SOC businesses actually pick up at the times that they're the busiest. They are able to make better use of their time because they have so much to fit in, and so they schedule it and get it done!

Reevaluate your why and your priorities, organize your time, and fit in whatever activities you can manage on a consistent basis. Don't tell someone how "busy" you are! Forget it—excuses SOC!

LUCKY SOCS

Do you know people you consider to be lucky? Well if you believe in the law of attraction and positivity and momentum, it's not surprising that what you perceive as luck is able to be controlled and even conjured up.

Benjamin Franklin once said that "Diligence is the mother of good luck." Isn't it great to know that you can have a say in how lucky you are by doing the right things to bring it on? I read an article a while ago from a website called "Give More," by Sam Parker, which contained some bullet points about improving your luck; I wasn't surprised to see that it echoed all the concepts that I've always taught my team about how to effectively increase their positive results. So here are just a few ways to bring on that luck in your SendOutCards business, so you can bask in the golden glow at the end of the rainbow!

First, do the work and be ready for the opportunities that come your way. Take initiative and learn the website. You don't have to know everything right away. But if you want to do this business, it's important that when someone asks you a question you don't know the answer to, *find it.* Be curious, read what's on the site, read the FAQ, the site index, watch the system trainings, and read what your upline sends you. This is your responsibility, not theirs.

As in any job, there is no way you're going to know everything on the first day. One summer during a college break I worked at the front desk at the YMCA, and I was terrified to answer the phones! I didn't know anything yet, and I felt like no matter what someone asked me, I wouldn't be able to answer, and I hated that feeling. After two weeks or so, I was a pro. I loved answering the phones, I loved coming to work, and I loved calling everyone by name.

This business is a process, and you don't have to know everything to get started. But if there are things you still don't know very well, make it your priority to ask more questions, read more, and figure it out. Being prepared will help you get to the next level, going from just enjoying your business to being really, really good at your business.

Next, really be alert and listen to the people, events, and things around you. Hone your SOC Ears! Take an interest in people. Don't just look for how something can benefit you. Strike up conversations with people you wouldn't normally talk to.

And of course, look for those reasons to send cards. How many heartfelt cards have you sent? Are you really sending one every day or are you just saying you do? How many cards have you sent to someone you don't know very well, or someone you just met?

Keep a pad of paper in your purse or at your desk and when something happens that you want to respond to, jot it down and take a moment to act on it later that day or evening. This business is about relationships. Not only are we showing people how **they** can build relationships, we are building our own relationships every day.

We have to walk our own walk! How can you be an advocate for cards if you don't send them? Jordan Adler once said that success in this business is almost directly proportionate to what people send out in cards and gifts. It goes hand in hand. People can't help asking about the cards or being touched by the cards when you send them in a heartfelt way. Trust your instincts, be genuine, and really show people why they will love it.

Next, be sure to make yourself open and available to new experiences. Get out of your comfort zone and take risks. One of the main reasons people think they can't "do" SOC is because they think, "Oh, I'm not a salesperson." In SOC, you don't have to be a salesperson. But you do have to sometimes explore outside your comfort zone.

Maybe chat with the person next to you on an airplane whereas normally you would put on your headphones. Ask people questions. Join a networking group. I remember my second day in SOC, I reached out and called my friend Angela; I knew she had a candle business, and all I knew was that she just **had** to see this.

She saw it, liked it, and said, "You should join my networking group." Icy fear took over, and I thought, "I don't know what that is, I don't know what I'd have to do, I don't know what I'd wear." All those thoughts came flooding into my head and I opened my mouth and said, "Sure, where is it?"

I jumped in, way out of my comfort zone, and joined a group of 30 business professionals who all came to the lunch from work, while I had just come straight from my pajamas at home. I jumped in and started sharing this system that I didn't really know anything about but knew that they needed it for their businesses and personal life. All of them started using it, and many of them are business builders on my team today.

What can you do to put yourself out there? Maybe it's a social event that normally you would skip but you think, "Well, maybe I'll meet someone interesting there." You don't know where things may lead. It is a vulnerable thing to put yourself out there and talk to new people and show them something where they may reject you. But once you start realizing that **this** is a business where people will **thank you** for showing it to them, it gets less scary.

Finally, really take action! Every time you feel stuck or down, go do a walkthrough or send a heartfelt card. It works to get you out of yourself.

And always try to manage your attitude. There are so many ups and downs in a business where you're your own boss, and you don't have control over who gets a package and who builds a team. Being positive will hugely increase your chances of having waves of luck that flow your way. I have seen time after time how someone's mindset affects their results.

Even if they don't think they're in a negative mindset, all the little comments they make, such as, "And of course, they didn't like it!" Or, "They said they don't have any money, surprise, surprise." It's that learned optimism again. If you are expecting the results to be negative, you are just letting it be confirmed and yes, you knew you'd fail, so you get to be right. I have also seen, time after time, examples of when people make up their mind to do something, and **they do it.**

I've seen distributors who decide that they want to promote before a Treat'em Right Seminar or other event, so they'll suddenly sign up six distributors in less than a week. They decide they're going to do this, and they do. One distributor decided that she was going to be Senior Manager before she went to a trade show so that she could wear the name tag I bought her, and she signed up 10 distributors in a week and a half!

One distributor decided he was going to become Senior Manager by the convention, so he bought his ticket to the Annual Convention in Salt Lake City, and signed up nine distributors in two weeks, the last one the evening before the convention started, while we were all sitting in the bar at 10:30 p.m.

One distributor went on a road trip over the summer with her two kids. She signed up four distributors, reaching the rank of Senior Manager, while she was traveling all over and fitting walkthroughs in amidst her trip. She even met one prospect in a gas station parking lot when she found out they were near the same exit!

Another Senior Manager was determined to win the SOC Stars trip, so she signed people up until midnight, up to the cutoff, and won. She set her mind to it, and she did it.

There are stories after stories like this. Why does this happen? Because they decide they have a goal, they know they're going to reach it, and they do it! And there isn't a single thought in their head that is telling them they can't or they're not going to reach it. It is very rare that you hear about someone setting his or her mind that strongly to something and failing. Why? Because you get what you focus on.

Now, does this momentum last forever? Not always. Some of these people reached their immediate goal and then went back to signing people up "once in a while." But what does that teach us? That you **can**—you could do it every day, if you want to.

So what does this mean for you? What do you want? Do you believe you can have it? Make up your mind that **today** is the day for it. And go after it. It works. And when you fail sometimes (which we all do) learn something from it and continue on in a smarter way. That is the **key** to this business. We all hear "no." We all make mistakes. We all have ups and downs. The success is in when you **continue** on, and continually learn from your journey. Back to that YMCA job—there is always a learning curve. And no one is perfect from day one. But if you keep going in this business, you can't help but succeed.

And luckily for us, in SOC there is nothing to "quit" anyway. SOC is like buying a couch. You can pretend you don't have it anymore, but it's still sitting in your living room!

We are sharing products with others that are less expensive than those in the marketplace. We are using our tool every day to make people's lives better. When we come across someone who hasn't heard of it, we share it with them to see if they want to use it to make their life better. And we're showing people a fun and enjoyable way to make income and create financial freedom. Why would you stop doing that?

So you will succeed. When you show this to people, your business moves forward. When you don't, it won't. But if you want faster growth, set your goals—and make your own luck.

LET EVERY TIME
BE THE FIRST TIME

The longest period of time that I ever played a particular role in a musical was the national and international tour of *The Sound of Music*, which toured for over a year throughout the United States, Canada, Korea, Singapore, Bangkok, and Hong Kong. I was "Maria," the Julie Andrews role, and basically never left the stage for the entire three hours. Sometimes we had as many as eight or nine shows a week. It was grueling, yet wonderful!

One of the questions I always got was, "How can you do the same show night after night?" People wanted to know if I got tired of saying the same lines and singing the same songs. An actor who merely goes through the motions is commonly referred to as "phoning it in," which makes it difficult for an audience to really connect to what they're doing because they're almost imitating themselves, instead of experiencing the emotions of the character. It was important to me to never let that happen.

The truth is that no, I didn't ever get tired of doing that show, night after night. And the reason was this: every night when I sat on that rock in my nun costume behind the curtain and listened to the orchestra tune up, I completely forgot about everything except for living life through my character's eyes, and actually experiencing her journey as it was happening.

Every single night onstage as "Maria," I left the Abbey, became a governess to seven spunky children, fought for what I believed in, fell in love with a captain, questioned my choices, sought advice, got married, and escaped from Austria! I threw myself into the role as if it was all happening for the very first time, each and every time.

That's the only way you can do the same thing over and over without it getting stale. You have to live it as if it's the first time for yourself, **and** you get to live it through the eyes of the audience, which actually **is** seeing it for the first time.

Even the times when I was exhausted, or had a two-show day, or had just traveled eight hours on a bus to the next city and couldn't even imagine doing a three-hour, high-energy show, I grounded myself, focused on what I had to do, and lived the journey as if it was the first time I ever said those lines or felt those emotions.

In SendOutCards, it's exactly same thing. If you are working this business, then you will probably be sharing this tool and business opportunity hundreds and hundreds of times. Even though you're using automated tools, like the opportunity video and the walkthrough with Kody, if you let yourself get into the state where you're bored by it, this will come across to the person you're sharing it with. You have to get in the mindset that it's **their** first time seeing it, and they deserve the very best.

Live it through their eyes each time you're showing it. Enjoy helping them pick out a card to send to someone they care about, and feel proud when they "ooh!" and "ahh!" when they see the gifts. Experience all the reasons along with them that this will save them time and money, and have fun sharing how much you enjoy the business.

It's as if you were to take your best friend to a place you love that he's never seen before; you get so much enjoyment out of seeing **him** enjoy it, even if you've been there yourself many times before.

BE YOUR OWN BEST YOU

Don't imitate someone else. If you're not perky, don't be perky. Don't use someone else's jokes. Be true to yourself. Find what works for you within your personality and framework, and it will ring true to the people with whom you are sharing it.

There are many, many different personalities and characters who have achieved success in this business. You don't ever have to be a cookie-cutter of someone else. Glean ideas from people, but then find the style that you connect to personally and feel comfortable doing, and make it your own.

DON'T EXPECT TO FEEL MAGICALLY DIFFERENT

Most people can think of someone else that they'd like their business to look like. Some people have expressed to me that they'd love to be where I am in my business. I would love to be where Adam and Jeff Packard are. They may want to be where Jim Packard is. Jim may want to be where Jordan Adler is. I remember asking Adam once, "When did you feel like it really started taking off for you?" And he said "I still don't feel like it has." And that really struck me.

Really? With all of his distributors, he didn't hit that point where it felt like a runaway train? But the thing is, your "bar" keeps shifting too. And though there was a time when you thought making $500 a month would be good, one day that won't be quite good enough, and you'll be wanting to make $2,000 a month. Or you'll want to have 5,000 distributors instead of 500.

Even Jordan Adler would like things to be moving faster, though any of us would be happy to trade our check for his, I'm sure! But because your internal bar keeps going up, that's why it seems like only a little bit is happening every day. You'll always want to be further along, but that's okay. Let that drive you, not discourage you. Slow and steady is okay. It's still growth. And always try to recognize how far you've come and what your accomplishments have been, even if you now want to be somewhere else down the line.

LET THEM WEAR SOCKS...OR NOT!

It's not all on you to say the perfect thing to "get someone to see" why they should do this business. When you really internalize that, it will lift the pressure right off you. The right person will see this opportunity and go for it, regardless of how knowledgeable or convincing you are. The wrong person won't do anything no matter what. There are people you have yet to meet who will "get it" too. Getting into activity is what matters most, so you can get it in front of the most people.

The next "Jordan Adler" could be sponsored by someone who barely even knows how to put a photo into a card. The right person will see the opportunity and run toward it, not away from it. If they have questions along the way, they'll call you, not the other way around.

Think about how much cajoling and pressuring and help the person in your upline had to give you to get you to start doing something—probably not very much, right? Similarly take a look at your downline so far, and write down the names of all of your Senior Managers, Managers, and any distributor who is working the business without your constant coaxing.

Now think back to how long it took them to sign up after seeing the walkthrough for the first time. If they're below your first level and you're not sure, go ahead and ask them. I think you'll find that most of those people signed up on the spot or within two or three days of seeing this opportunity.

If you have to convince and coax someone, and overcome every tiny objection in their mind, then yes, they may eventually sign up. You can get pretty good at reassuring your prospects in that moment that it's something they should do. Yet since you won't be able to camp out on their shoulder continually, chances are they'll immediately revert back to all their own fears and objections and self-talk, and they'll end up really not doing much of anything.

Successful people constantly feed their minds and souls with personal development training and ideas that will help them continually grow in their journey. And yet the people who would benefit from those ideas the most have no curiosity or hunger to do the same.

Have you ever seen a really thin person working out like a maniac and think, "Why do they need to work out so much—they're already so thin!" But then you think, "Oh, they're probably so thin because they work out." Hmmm.

Now, I'm not saying you should throw out someone's business card just because he didn't sign up on the spot. Of course you should still follow up with your new shiny magic sentence. Many of the people whom I followed up with consistently are using the system today and even referring it periodically to others.

But don't devote huge amounts of energy toward convincing people. If you have to go way off your normal path of simple follow-up to try to drag someone, it's probably not going to be a match...for either of you.

Most of the leaders in this company needed very little help to get started doing what we're doing. You can't say the wrong thing to the right person, so spend your time going out and finding those people who see the value of what you're offering. You can change the world, but you can't save the world.

If they don't want to wear socks, let them be cold!

WALK THE SOC WALK

If you had ever told me a few years ago that I was going to leave New York City, move to Florida, and send 8,000 greeting cards, I would have thought you'd gone completely mad. But yes, I've sent out over 8,000 cards in three years. I don't even think about it. It's what I do. I constantly send unexpected birthday cards, gifts, nice to meet you cards, unexpected cards. Any time I think "I should do this," I do it! I promise you, you'll get more interest and leads out of the unexpected cards that you send out than from almost any other source.

If you're thinking that 8,000 cards sounds like a lot, don't worry. It's not like I started my SOC business and instantly started sending thousands of cards! As your success grows, you'll start to send more and more. This is not a business where you have to spend millions of dollars in order to be successful.

If you're not on the $31 subscription, however, ask yourself: In what kind of business you can be really successful where you're not willing to spent at least $31 a month on your own marketing? Cards and gifts are your business. How can you represent something if you're not fully a product of the product?

Look for reasons to send cards and gifts every single day. My husband Jeremy once sent a box of 16 brownies to the entire pharmacy department at Target, because they were always so helpful and friendly to him every time he went in there. Do you think they ever hear how great they are from people, or do you think they mainly receive complaints? Yeah, good guess!

Now, every time he goes back in there, one of them shouts exuberantly, "It's the brownie guy!" And they all gather around and greet him and smile. He didn't do this to "get them" into my business; he just wanted to express his sincere appreciation. Maybe they'll ask about it when he sends another card some time, or maybe not, but he certainly feels like a rockstar every time he goes into Target, that's for sure!

People in a store, customer service reps on the phone, waiters who went above and beyond, friends you haven't seen in a while, acquaintances you meet at a networking event—people are people, and they want to feel appreciated. Use humor, be creative and let your cards and gifts be shining examples of why they should care about using this system themselves and being a part of something really special.

WAIT FOR NOTHING!

It is so easy to find yourself waiting in this business:

Waiting for that one person who keeps saying that they are going to sign up but haven't yet.

That distributor who signs up and does nothing.

That company who's waiting to ask their boss and said they'll get back to you.

The person who says they want to sign up but have no money.

The person who says they're going to talk to a bunch of people first and let you know if they want to sign up based on their reaction!

Another magic sentence to live by is: **Wait for nothing!** *Let everything happen on the way to something else.*

Last December, there was a prospect with whom I did a walkthrough of the system, and afterwards he said he really liked it, but he was going to talk to some people to see if anyone was interested before he signed up. I tried to discourage him from doing that, explaining that it doesn't really work that way, and that you can't just describe this to people. You have to walk them through sending a card with a gift account to truly understand the value.

But he was insistent that that's how he'd know if other people "wanted this" and he didn't want to sign up until he had a line of people saying "Yes, here's my credit card." Well, what can you do, right? So then I couldn't get him on the phone, and kept following up for months, and finally I talked to him in March, and he said dismissively, "Oh yeah, I talked to a bunch of people and no one was interested."

So while we were talking, I pulled up my back office genealogy and I saw that **since my walkthrough with him,** I'd had 110 people come into my downline. And I couldn't help thinking, "Wow, that's such a shame that no one you talked to was interested, but that's probably because that's not the way to work this business!" A hundred and ten distributors signed up while he was busy proving to himself (the wrong way) that no one wanted it.

Well, thank goodness I wasn't waiting around for him to sign up, and putting my business on hold. No one person is going to make or break your business. Even if they have a lot of contacts or tell you that they're going to do great things, move on and sign people up—let their actions speak, not their words.

The worst thing you can do is wait for someone else to do anything. Maybe it's the glass half-empty in me, but you know what? I'd rather keep on going and be pleasantly surprised if they actually do.

So you've done a walkthrough for someone, and you follow up, and you're waiting, and you're overcoming their objections, and you're waiting, and you're talking to them, and you're convincing them, and you're dragging them and you're begging them and you're sending them cards galore, and you're sending them statistics and writing long emails and calling them some more... Well, guess what? You could have showed 10 other people that walkthrough in the same amount of time!

Here's another magic sentence, for those of you who love alliteration as much as I do: *Keep filling your pipeline with people or you'll plunge into a pothole!*

The minute you find yourself frustrated with someone, it means you are putting **way** too much weight on whether they're a yes or a no. Remember, everything needs to happen on the way to something else. Your socks can have holes, but it won't slow you down!

Be organized, but have 100 balls in the air. Always remember one of my all-time favorite magic sentences: *No one wants to get on your bus if you're driving in a circle!*

Set your sights on your destination and go! Don't let anyone derail you—that momentum absolutely will carry you through.

Have some good points when you show them the system, tell them why you love it, give them some ideas of how they can use it or what the business can do for them, and show them the ways to get started. That's it!

Now that doesn't mean you don't need to follow up, because often someone really does want it, but they won't actually sit down and do it until you call two or three times and they say, "Oh okay, I'm ready. Let's do this now."

But you cannot spend all your time and energy on one person. And in SOC, the great news is that you don't have to.

There are a zillion more people that you could be showing this to around the corner. If you get bogged down by one, you will accomplish nothing.

And the other interesting fact is that they can sense it. If you are waiting and waiting and waiting for that one person, how scary is that for them? They can feel that you're waiting for them and it makes people nervous to feel that they are responsible for your success. And do **they** want a business that seems to rest on only one person? Your job is to follow up consistently and persistently but then move on and do another walkthrough here, and another follow-up call there, again and again.

If you have enough numbers in the pipeline, you also won't put as much pressure on what happens with each one. Just do the walkthrough, send a follow-up email, send a thank-you card, make those follow-up calls—and repeat. Attach the importance to the activity, not the result. When your pipeline is full, the right people will fall in line and say "yes" to the opportunity.

And for those of you who think that no one else has the problems and objections that you're encountering, think again. These things happen to everyone! We all hear these words from people:

"I'm really busy."

"I can't find anyone to ask."

"Everyone says they have no money."

We all hear every objection in the world of why they can't get set up with a package right now or they can't work the business. But being a leader means that you don't wait and let all of that slow you down.

Your business will **never** be broken by a "no." Or a whole string of "no's!" It's only broken if you stop asking the question.

THE "OTHER" LILY PAD STORY

You've probably heard the quiz question in network marketing about the lily pad and the pond:

> If a single lily pad doubles every day throughout the month of June, beginning June 1, and continues to double until the entire pond was covered, what percentage of the pond will be completely covered with lily pads on the 29th day?

The answer is 50 percent, which is such a dramatic and valuable lesson of the power of exponential growth.

Well, my lily pad analogy is slightly different, and it's much more "aerobic!" So imagine that every time you do a walk-through, it's like stepping onto a lily pad while you're trying to cross a wide pond. When people are positive and excited about what you're showing them, it's a fluffy lily pad that keeps you afloat. When people are negative, and don't call you back, and dilly-dally around, they represent the "sloggy" lily pads that sink under your weight and try to drag you deep down into the murky swamp. (Yes, I made up the word sloggy, but that's just because it really fits!)

So what can you do? It's your job to simply leap lightly from buoyant lily pad to buoyant lily pad, and if you land on a sinking sloggy one, get off **fast**—and do what it takes to get to a good one again.

You will definitely hit the sloggy sinkholes periodically, and you will experience those droopy lily pads trying to drag you under, until you're consumed by the nearby alligators, never to utter the words "PicturePlus 2.0" again.

But leap off those hazardous pads as quickly as possible at the first sign of sinkage, and get to the next one that will hold you up and support you. Over time you will propel yourself steadily and successfully to your destination.

DON'T EAT THE SCRAPS

One of my favorite magic sentences is actually in reference to dating. For whatever reason, I seem to be the person that friends come to for sage relationship advice over the years. They get a kick out of my funny stories and guidelines to follow, so somewhere along the way, they coined the term "Jules' Rules."

There are undeniably some rumors that Jules' Rules have resulted in several marriages, rescued some from impending heartbreak, and provided courage to a few brave souls as they ventured into the tangled web of internet dating. I'm just sayin'! Following Jules' Rules leads to a much higher chance of achieving a successful long-term relationship!

My magic phrase "Don't Eat the Scraps" applies to that precarious time period within the first six to eight weeks of a new relationship, when everyone tends to screw it up. I have almost single-handedly saved many blossoming relationships from plunging fatally into imminent disaster as quickly as they began. I wish I could fill you in on the details of the magic rule, but alas, since this book has nothing to do with dating whatsoever, I'm afraid you'll just have to wait until *Jules' Rules* hits the shelves!

I will say this though: Don't eat the SOC scraps either. Many people will talk a great game when they sign up. They will tell you how many people they're going to sponsor, how many connections they have, or how well they've done in another business. They'll tell you they're going to advance to Executive in four weeks.

They'll tell you they're going to "bring over" their 30,000 people from another downline. They'll tell you they're going to do all the things **you** always did anyway, without ever having had the need to announce to someone that you were going to do them.

Don't eat those scraps. Don't look at them. Don't pick them up and inspect them. Don't sniff in their general direction. Let those little suckers whiz past your head without a single glance or acknowledgement. At the end of that crucial scrap-flinging period, (you'll know when it's safe to emerge!), if they are still present, still dedicated, seemingly coachable, and have made noticeable strides toward a few of their claims, well, then you just may have something here.

But you will save yourself a lot of disappointment if you can just resist the temptation to buy into all the "almosts" and "what ifs" and "just wait until I's" and "it would have been so"...Yeah. It would have.

Go forth and be scrap-resistant!

WE ALL PAY
THE SAME DUES

Have you ever found yourself looking at your upline or a leader in this business, and you think "Oh, they don't know what it's like, they don't have my problems?" Well, dust off your class ring and think back to those college years.

In a fraternity or sorority, the freshmen feel like "Gee, I can't wait to be a senior—they're so lucky, they have it easy. I have to do all the grunt stuff and they get to enjoy the rewards."

But there's still an underlying understanding that the seniors started out as freshmen themselves at one point, and they went through the exact same thing when *they* were freshmen. Just because they are where they are now, and it may be more fun, that doesn't mean they didn't have to do all the hard stuff to get there.

In a fraternity, the seniors purposely make the freshmen's lives hell—mostly because *they* had to go through hell!

So now consider network marketing for a second. In a network marketing company, we try to make everything better for those who are coming after us. We want to encourage them, shorten their learning curve, help them get where we are—faster.

Once someone starts to do well in SendOutCards, why do they start leading conference calls and newsletters and team events? To help provide everyone else with the tools they've learned as well. The leaders in SOC spend **a lot** of time and energy helping others to succeed. And yet for some reason, yet again, people are just bound and determined to believe that certain people who have achieved success are lucky.

When an unknown actor gets a big part in a movie, what we do all call it? A lucky break! And we all act like this person came from nowhere. I probably wasn't the only person thinking that when *Jerry Maguire* first came out. I had never heard of Renee Zellweger, and I remember watching her in a role with Tom Cruise and thinking, "Who the heck is this girl and where on earth did she come from?"

One of my friends, John Lloyd Young, won the Tony Award for his leading role as "Frankie Valli" in *Jersey Boys* on Broadway. He is the only American actor in history at this time to receive a Lead Actor in a Musical Tony, Drama Desk, Outer Critics Circle and Theatre World Award for a Broadway debut. Everyone was saying, "Where did he come from?"

I'll tell you where he came from: An office on 49th and Broadway where he transcribed for news networks alongside me and about 30 other people, while going off on tour periodically to do children's theater to keep his health insurance!

And get this: Although he had auditioned for it, he didn't even get the part originally in the pre-Broadway run of *Jersey Boys*! They gave it to someone else. Did he stop there? No, he knew it was for him, and he kept auditioning. A year later, he was given the role when it officially opened on Broadway. "Lucky" break?

Throughout my 12 years as a professional singer and actress in New York City, I faced more rejection than most of you could possibly imagine! I'd get up at 5 a.m. and wait out on the street next to the trash for three hours in the freezing cold in New York City, just to finally get inside and sign up for a two-minute audition slot later in the day. I'd go to my transcription job, type until my audition, and then trek back to the studio, where we were herded in a huge line like cattle in order of our scheduled appointment time.

One by one, we'd go into the room, put the music down in front of the bored pianist, and sing 16 magnificent bars (which lasts about one minute, tops) and smile at the blank-faced panel of directors and choreographers, who dismiss you with a curt, "Thank you!"

So there was nothing to do except leave and then you never hear anything again until one day you hear that the cast has started rehearsals, so it's pretty safe to say you're not in it.

For 12 years I did this. Why? Does this sound fun? Well, we do it because we believe in ourselves, we love it, we believe that someone else will see what we see in ourselves. When you have a dream like that, no amount of rejection or lack of work makes people say, "Okay, well forget it."

Can you imagine someone moving to New York City to pursue their dream of a performing career, going to three or four auditions without success, and then moving back home saying,

"Oh well, I gave it a shot!" Would you think that they had given it a fair try?

And of course in between all the rejections are the times when you do get cast in a show, when someone lets you do what you do best. And for that three months or one year or however long it lasts, you are one of the "lucky ones," getting paid to do what you love to do. And then you're right back where you started, in line at 5 a.m. again.

In SOC, the "successful" people have faced every single obstacle that you've ever faced and more, but they kept moving through the lily pads to leap off the sloggy, icky ones to get to the ones that keep them inspired, and keep them remembering their why in the first place. They come off each success or failure, and get back in line to continually work toward their goal.

Have you noticed that you feel like you're only as good as your last good walkthrough or presentation!? The minute you sign someone up, you're on top of the world, and you love SOC and everything's awesome. And then you go through a string of **no** signups, and no one likes it and no one does what they say they're going to do, and your whole energy changes. "This is hard." "I hate everyone!" Or "Maybe I'm not good at this." There's that learned optimism explanatory style again.

In SendOutCards, they say you must have a strong belief system. But what does that mean? It means that no amount of what anyone else says will make you say "Okay, never mind. Forget it." No amount of no's, no amount of objections, questions, indecision, teasing, or ignorant questions about pyramids will make you walk away from this business that you believe in.

How strong is your belief? How strong is your "why" and your mission and your belief in this company and where it is going… and **your role** in it? It's truly not the things that happen to you **but how you deal with them** that counts in this business.

I used to think that all that personal development stuff was so inconsequential. "You need to work more on yourself than on your business." What? No thank you, I'm fine! What the heck are they talking about?

But I understand that now. It gives you that vocabulary for dealing with setbacks. We **all** have the same opportunity video, the same walkthrough, the same Daily 8 and Fast Start CDs, the same amount of time in the day. So what makes us different? Our perseverance, our belief, our positivity, our inner voice. Be the person that takes charge, doesn't wait, doesn't make excuses, and leads others. You cannot underestimate the strength of how all of that will carry you through from one lily pad to the next.

HAVE A LOT OF
SOCKS IN THE AIR

I generally do not try to "close" on the spot when I'm sharing SOC with someone. If someone loves this and sees the value of it, they'll go ahead with it whether they do it immediately or sometime in the future. But you have to have an organized system for follow-up. It is an absolute certainty that the one area where people really, really drop the ball on is calling their prospects back. It is a human tendency to start telling yourself that if you haven't heard from them, they must not be interested.

Well, start telling yourself that **everyone** is interested. The last time you talked to them on the phone, they oohed and aahed and crooned and said they loved it, but then you can't get them on the phone and you've called five times and feel like an idiot, so you stop. And then what? You are putting in your own head what they're thinking.

You know what I think to myself? I think, "The last time I talked to them, they loved it, and I'm going to keep following up until they tell me otherwise!" Why not? I'm going off the information they gave me. I'm not going to let the fact that I haven't heard from them morph into, "They think I'm stalking them."

And I know for a fact that sometimes it's been three months, six months, seven months when someone finally says, "Okay, I'm ready now. Thank you so much for being patient!" I help people get the system on their time frame, not mine. Everyone really does like it. Why wouldn't they? And why wouldn't they want to get set up with at least one of the packages, if not become a distributor?

So I'm just going to call them on their time frame, and be helpful (not pushy) until they're ready. If you don't, one day someone else will bring it up to them and they'll say "Oh yeah, SOC—I really liked it, but that girl stopped calling me!" And they will absolutely not remember that you called them 143 times. It will be their sole recollection that you *stopped* calling them.

When successful people have signups consistently, it's not necessarily because they're signing up the same people that they just did a presentation for that day. They're not so "lucky" that everyone who sees the system hypnotically pulls out their credit card and says, "Yes, yes, oh wise one, please help me build a team of thousands!"

The secret to signing people up consistently is to have a million balls in the air, follow up, wait for nothing. And no matter what, don't let any number of no's slow you down.

when SOC-ortunity *knocks*

THERE'S NO PLACE LIKE HOME

I had never been a huge fan of home or hotel meetings in network marketing. In fact, I was initially even more drawn to SOC as a business because you didn't have to do home parties to share it, and there weren't any meetings you had to go to.

It's a business where you can work from home, show someone the system one-on-one, and anyone can benefit from it; it wasn't a "rah-rah, get everyone riled up and trick 'em into signing up for something with no substance" kind of business.

Well, although I will always continue to do one-on-one walkthroughs to show people this business and tool, recently my feelings about meetings has changed completely. This is an amazing business with an amazing income opportunity that changes people's lives, and I had no reason not to sing it from the rooftops. Once I started doing home opportunity meetings, I was thrilled to find that it didn't feel salesy and awkward—it simply felt like another chance to show the tool and the business for something I'm passionate about.

After all, I'm just showing them what I've been doing all this time and why I love it. If nothing else, at least they'll see what it is, since most people still don't know. And at the very best, they'll see the value in it as well.

I found that my old reluctance to delve into home parties and meetings doesn't extend to SOC because of the subject matter. And there is great value in showing the tool to several people at once, having them see the social proof that others love it, being surrounded by fun, positive people, and seeing the actuality of what kind of support they'll be plugging *their* guests into if they join.

There is definite momentum in gathering people together who are excited by the same things. It's like that "You Tube" video of the guy dancing crazily in the middle of the field, and then one by one, people stepped up to join him until everyone was doing it, and it was the people on the sides who seemed like the party-poopers.

My home meetings just didn't feel like one of those things that I always disliked and avoided. Why? Because I love SOC. And I love sharing SOC. And there's nothing wrong with sharing it with a lot of people at once. You can help a brand new distributor get started right away by helping to share the opportunity with their friends and prospects.

Plus, joint meetings take the onus off of feeling that you need to find a million people all the time to sign up personally. Doing one-on-ones sometimes puts the pressure on you to sign up a lot of people by yourself, whereas doing group meetings is really about finding a few who bring a few who bring a few, which is truly what network marketing is all about. We aren't in sales. If we were, we could make a good salary "selling" this, but never a great salary, which is what makes this industry so attractive.

I often hear from distributors who are frustrated because they feel like they're dragging people. You will exhaust yourself and burn yourself out by dragging people or doing everything yourself. Starting regular meetings will help with this.

Put events in place and grow a steady place and a positive environment for your team to grow: conference calls, small group meetings, newsletters, group gatherings. Promote the next event at your current event, and people will feel like they have a supportive place to bring guests and grow without having to know everything themselves.

Of course, never stop doing those great one-on-ones, because you have the ability to share SOC every day in 25 minutes! Don't wait for the meetings to show it to someone. Do both. Why not give yourself another way to share it? What's not to like about a meeting where several distributors sign up at once, and you're helping other team members do the same?

MONEY IN THE SOC DRAWER

SendOutCards is simply fantastic, hands-down, and almost all of us would use it anyway, even if we weren't paid to share it, right? But in addition to enjoying the use of this tool to make our lives better, what else do we want? We want to find people who see our vision, who want to actively share this opportunity with others. Repeat after me: *We want to find people who see our vision, who want to actively share this opportunity with others.*

If everyone who signed up as a distributor then proceeded to share this with a few others in their lives, who then did the same, and so on and so on, our teams would just grow and grow, right? (Wistful sigh!)

It's not too surprising that if you talk about the SOC tool to others, you'll attract a lot of customers. But if you talk about the opportunity, you'll attract business builders who want to change their current situation.

We all have glorified "customers" in our downline; people who made the choice to sign up as a distributor but then never shared it with anyone. This happens. It doesn't mean you're doing something wrong as a leader. That's life. Many people will see the value of the entrepreneur package, but for various reasons will not go on to work their business. Don't forget, we get paid every month on the volume of cards and gifts being sent, so it's okay if there are people in our business who simply use the tool and who enjoy sending cards!

But ultimately we are not in the business of sales. We are a network marketing company. In the long run, we all want to benefit from the time-leveraging that our business model is based upon. We can't be scared about sharing with others that this is a great business that really can and will change one's financial future.

Why are we nervous to tell people about an opportunity? Because it would mean that they would have to spend money before they can start making money? Yeah...and? Name one business that you can start for free, out of thin air? Our initial outlay to start our SOC enterprise is *nothing* when, in return, we receive a business with everything in place, with which we can start making money right away.

Even a $500 or $1,000 investment wouldn't have been a lot, not for everything we're getting. We are all familiar with other businesses with a similar structure to ours, where by the time you've bought all their products and kits and samples, etc., you've spent a couple thousand dollars to get started.

And don't forget those traditional business models, where you have to lay down hundreds of thousands of dollars to start a brick and mortar business, which won't even show a glimmer of a profit for years while it's getting off the ground. Our opportunity is nothing like that!

I always enjoy hearing Kody Bateman talk about how **his** distributorship didn't cost $457. His "entrepreneur package" cost $500,000 to start SendOutCards. How lucky are we! For a minimal startup fee, we're able to have our own business, representing an amazing tool, where everything is already in place for us, that allows us to ultimately replace our current incomes and create financial freedom, just by telling people it exists. Sounds pretty fair to me.

Another big worry we have when sharing this opportunity is that people "wouldn't be interested." One of my new distributors, as an explanation for why he hadn't shown SOC to anyone after he signed up said to me, "The problem is that I live in an affluent community, and some of these people make a couple hundred thousand dollars a year."

Well, fantastic! Those are the people that already have a successful money blueprint. T. Harv Eker wrote a wonderful book called *Secrets of the Millionaire Mind*, outlining how you already have a personal relationship with money ingrained in your subconscious mind, and that ultimately determines how successful you will be financially.

Whether it was formed through influences from your childhood, your own limiting beliefs, or your past history with money, if your money blueprint is not set for a high level, you will never achieve true financial success. (Don't worry—you can work to reset your money blueprint if it's not where it needs to be!)

Therefore, these affluent people who have created success in their lives thus far are even more likely than most to see the incredible entrepreneurial value of this business. Not to mention that perhaps their successful career requires them to work long hours away from their family. Maybe they are, in fact, quite miserable doing what it is they do, but they don't believe that they have any other choice to continue supporting their current lifestyle. Most importantly, if they stopped working or something prevented them from doing what they're doing, how long would their money last?

It really resonated with me when I first heard that the definition of wealth is not determined by how much money you earn at your job, the clothes you wear, or the kind of lifestyle you lead. The true definition of wealth is how long a period of time you can sustain your current lifestyle if you stopped working. When you factor in your expenses, your assets, and your passive income, you find out how "rich" you really are, based on how long you could last. That's a sobering thought, isn't it?

Have you ever been surprised to learn that a lawyer or doctor that you know is working a network marketing business on the side? Whether we admit it or not, we all have preconceived ideas of who "should" and "shouldn't" be building a "business like that."

Just because an individual is already making good money or has savings in the bank doesn't mean he or she isn't entitled to achieve financial freedom and more time with their families. Network marketing wasn't created for losers who aren't able to make money any other way! Network marketing is a model that attracts successful people who see the value in this industry, and want to work hard so that they can achieve their dreams and aspirations in life.

Does this mean that someone has to already have a lot of money to be successful in SendOutCards? Of course not! Another hugely successful personality type that we are all seeking as we grow our business is the entrepreneur with an unending drive, a strength of vision, and a belief in themselves that, despite any and all obstacles and situational limitations, they will succeed in reaching their goals!

The definition of the word entrepreneur is, *"A person who has possession of a new enterprise, venture or idea, and assumes significant accountability for the inherent risks and the outcome."*

The true entrepreneur needs no coaxing, training, reminding, or incentives, despite the "risks" of failing. They are driven by their own internal goals, and they will work this business with a fervor, once they set their minds to the fact that this is the vehicle that will to get them to their desired destination. Would you like a few people like this in your downline? I thought as much. Then never assume that someone wouldn't be interested until you show them the opportunity you're presenting.

Finally, we worry that people will look down on network marketing. Kody Bateman often speaks about the importance of strengthening your MLM Blueprint. This is crucial in taking your business to the next level. Your success in SOC hugely depends on being in full alignment with this industry and SOC's role within it.

One of the best books I've read recently is *The Business of the 21st Century*, where Robert T. Kiyosaki powerfully outlines how there is no better time than now to create genuine wealth, help to develop and build up others around you, and create a happier life in the process. The further and further into the book you delve, the more you will be reassured that you are on the right path, at the right time, with the right business that will take you there.

You are not **selling** SOC to people; you are sharing with them your vision, hopes and dreams, and how you can help them to attain theirs as well. It's not an empty promise, either. You represent a wonderful tool with a duplicatable system for success solidly in place, that provides the vehicle straight toward the financial freedom they seek.

Leading with the opportunity does not mean that you see other people as dollar signs. It means that you're looking for ways every day to help others to change their lives, as yours has been changed by the person who shared this with you. Imagine how different your life would be if he or she hadn't bothered to tell you about it!

Be genuine and true to yourself when sharing it with others. Paint the picture for where you're going, never tell your team to do something that you're not actively doing yourself, and do your best to support those who want to join you as you reach your goals together. The time to build your business and take control of your future is now! Don't leave the money in the drawer.

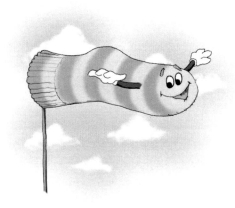

THE WIND BENEATH
YOUR WINDSOC

In a business where duplication is the key, I'd say we're all pretty lucky to have some incredible leaders to model our businesses after. Just like a sock with its multicolored pieces of yarn and textures, each leader in this company has a distinct personality, qualities, and behaviors, uniquely interwoven together.

We identify with and connect to various aspects of our different role models, and are strengthened and enriched by their example every day. We each embody a combination of these qualities as well, to form our own unique fabric of what we offer to the world. Whenever we recognize a familiar quality in someone else, it allows us to have the instant feeling of "I'm like that" or "That's me!" We are inspired by leaders when we see part of ourselves in them and experience that shared connection.

The best part about SOC is how different everyone is from each other! Imagine if there was only one model of what success looked like. Then only a select few would be able to identify with those at the top and envision themselves among them.

Let's open up our colorful **SOC Leaders Drawer** and look at the variety pack inside:

We have Jordan Adler, Eagle Distributor and currently the #1 income-earner in SOC, whose Monday night calls and overall leadership is insightful, practical, and inspirational. He constantly seeks out those who are doing something unique and special in their business, and then highlights, recognizes and shares it. He never coaches us to do anything that he is not also doing himself every day, leading by example. Jordan is a unique leader in that he is able to see both the big picture **and** the details, and is able to beautifully frame and convey his simple and inspiring message to others.

Eagle Distributor DeMarr Zimmerman is responsible for helping to create many of the systems and structures that we know in SOC today. He is the creator of the Fast Start CD and manual, which is a tool that instantly made this business even easier and more duplicable for us all. He also was instrumental in designing our incredible compensation plan, to set us all up for success. DeMarr's constant humor and tendency to play down his strengths make him endearing and relatable. Despite his vast knowledge of this industry, he allows everyone to feel that they too can do what he has accomplished.

David Frey is one of the most intelligent marketers you'll ever meet. After a 15-minute conversation with him you'll feel as if you've learned more than you could in a six-week course. He is typically contemplative and low-key, yet if you have the rare opportunity to hear him speak to an audience, he springs into dynamic action and delivers information that is always powerful and interesting. David inspires you to learn things that you didn't even know that you wanted to know!

Bob and Betty Ann Golden are vivacious and warm leaders, who work closely with their downline members to successfully create huge amounts of duplication in depth as well as width. This means that their "golden touch" extends far behind just their own arms' length. They are loving and fun, make a point to remember people's names, and never put themselves above others. They genuinely care about the people they already know, have just met, and those who have yet to come into their lives.

Jim Packard is honorable, funny, and thoughtful. He loves tracking and measuring activities and results, to constantly gather information and tweak its success rate. He was one of the main creators of our Daily 8 system, which helps us measure our progress and results. Jim is a huge proponent of keeping in touch with past and current clients and distributors, and he receives many referrals from people because of successfully maintaining those strong relationships. He keeps a good balance in his life and keeps his priorities in check. His love for his wife and sons is the glow that surrounds his every move, and it is proof that getting to work with the people you love is one of the best blessings you could ask for.

Jeff Packard is a smart and driven leader who seeks to create systems that are duplicatable and successful for his team to follow. He'll be the first one to come up with a plan, put it into action, and infuse it with consistency and purpose. He is fiercely loyal in both business and personal relationships.

Adam Packard, author of *Stay the Course*, is entrepreneurial, fun and a wonderful motivator. His trainings are always thoughtfully laid out, information-rich, and hugely inspirational. He was one of the first leaders I ever met in SOC, and he set the tone as a giving leader who takes an interest in helping to support the success of others, even when it doesn't directly benefit him. As a brand new rep, I deeply appreciated and respected this and knew immediately that this was something I wanted to emulate in my business.

Jimmy Dick is a nationally-known trainer and speaker, with extensive experience in consulting on and designing compensation and marketing plans for various companies. He played a big role in implementing our current SOC compensation plan, and he is a huge wealth of knowledge and resources. He is funny, endearing, and really pays attention to the things that happen around him. He can be found at many a Treat'em Right Seminar or event, patiently answering the eager questions of new and seasoned distributors alike, who want to glean more from his experiences about the ins and outs of the industry.

Diane Walker is kind, giving, and may appear shy at first to those that don't know her. She prefers to stay out of the limelight, in general. But the most undeniable factor surrounding Diane is that her team absolutely adores her and would do anything for her. Though she works primarily online and enjoys social networking, her business is extremely personal and she takes the time to meet, work with, encourage, and take the time to know, practically everyone. She is the last one to take credit for anything but the first person to step up to help or praise others.

Kathy Paauw is a smart, dedicated, and detail-oriented leader who goes above and beyond to make things go more smoothly for her team. She is constantly looking to implement new ideas that will leverage how she can be more effective and help others to do the same. Kathy has been in the Eagle's Nest and a top leader from day one, despite successfully juggling other work and family obligations. She happily lends her support whenever someone needs her, and strives to put helpful systems and information in place so that everyone may benefit from her efforts and energies.

Kody Bateman, CEO and Founder of SendOutCards, and author of *Promptings: Your Inner Guide to Making a Difference,* is a visionary with a powerful and passionate mission. He has a story that leaves no one untouched, a love of family that extends to everyone in this company, and an unrelenting spirit that allows him to always succeed in the face of adversity. Kody has always had a thirst for knowledge to seek out that which he does not know, to constantly evolve in both his business and his personal journey. This business we all hold as our own was born from strong roots, deep love, and a mission that extends far beyond any reach Kody could have achieved on his own, creating a legacy forever to come.

Now how's that for a drawer chock-full of incredible leaders with hugely varying systems, personalities, and motivations that drive them? There is something there for everyone to relate to, emulate, and learn from.

There's one important note however: You don't have to have a leader in your town or your state to be successful. The leaders aren't there to do it for you. They're there so you can see what works, give you something to model, and to use their experience as a guide. You can do this whether they're near you or not.

If you don't have a leader in your area, **be** the leader. You have all of the tools available to you **right now** to be just as successful as anyone ever has been. If you allow yourself to feel disadvantaged because you don't have someone leading meetings in your area, it will hugely impede your progress and your ability to shine.

In fact, sometimes having a big leader in your area may end up holding you back from being the leader you would have become. Be the person that others want to emulate. Consider this very carefully: If you want to be like the leaders that you admire, will you ever get there *just by following?*

The reason that not everyone is a leader is that it's hard to take those first steps. And sometimes it's scary and lonely to take those steps when you're afraid no one else will follow. But it's worth it for those who do. There is no limit to what you can accomplish.

So select liberally from the bountiful qualities that you admire in the Drawer of Leaders. You don't have to put on any socks that don't fit. Gather the things that make sense to you, that you relate to, and that help you become your best you.

As you learn and grow in your business, you will constantly weave new elements into your own existing pattern, to fortify your socks and to make them stronger, so that you can withstand the elements and be in the best position you can to reap the rewards to come.

WHAT'S IN YOUR SOC DRAWER?

Open your SOC Drawer and smell the cedar and the fresh potpourris. You are the master of your business and you control what you focus on. What resources do you draw on if you're feeling low? What books have you read that helped you? What quotes do you love? What is your answer if someone asks, "Why are you doing this business?" On your lowest day, what stops you from walking away? What did you read in this book that made you say, "Yes, that's me," or "I need to work on that?" What concepts or quotes resonated with you the most?

You get to pick and choose! Fill your SOC Drawer with the culture, the magic sentences, the relationships, the stories, the why, the how-to's, the lessons, the triumphs, the successes, the friendships, the experiences, the values, the ethics, and the journey… until it's overflowing!

No amount of no's will make you say "Okay, forget it!" No amount of setbacks will throw you. No number of grumbling "nay-sayers" will disappoint you. You are armed with your beliefs and your tools and your hopes and your visions.

All your dreams and goals are within your reach, and your life and business will be rich with the fulfillment that you seek and deserve.

Now, SOC it to 'em!

GLOSSARY

NEW WORDS FOR A CHANGED WORLD!

SOC-abulary – Phrases expressed through thoughts, feelings, and the written word that uplift and inspire people to new heights.

SOC-able – (adj.) When you see something and all you can think about is that it would make an amazing PicturePlus 2.0 card! (i.e. "That's so soc-able!")

SOC-cess – Achieving greatness in the best personal development journey ever!

SOC-a-holic – Self-proclaimed addict who cannot stop (and has absolutely no desire to stop) sending cards and gifts to those around them to make people feel good every single day.

SOC-scuses – The sad and flimsy excuses that people give you for why they can't do what you both know they should do, but won't.

SOC-itis – The paralyzing illness that makes you completely unable to get anything done whatsoever because all you want to do is send cards and gifts all day long while chuckling quietly to yourself in anticipation.

SOC-sation – The incredible feeling of being touched by an unexpected card and gift.

In-SOC-nia – The inability to sleep once SOC comes into your life because all you can think about is all the people who need it and haven't seen it yet.

SOC-ignition – The acknowledgment and attention happily bestowed upon awesome people who do awesome things, by being both a leader and servant to many, many others. Sometimes can lead to pangs. Beware.

SOC and Awe – To stun someone in their tracks with a heartfelt unexpected card that makes their day.

SendOutCards Ears – The ability to tap into your seventh sense; to listen and react to the things that happen around you every day, resulting in an entirely new and heightened level of communication.

Wood-SOC – A three-day music and card-sending festival where thousands of people gather every year to listen to rap music performed by Kody B, the Master MC!

ACKNOWLEDGEMENTS

I have so many people to thank, from the bottom of my heart; not only those that have come into my life since I began my SOC business three years ago, but also those who have been ongoing sources of positive influence, support and inspiration to me as a whole. You are the shining jewels in my sock drawer!

To my husband, Jeremy Hammond-Chambers, for his never-ending belief in me and constant source of encouragement. Your patience and unflagging support from that first day that I said "So, I've kind of started this...card thing," have allowed me to explore my true potential and passions and grow as a person. I love you!

To Roslyn Price, my mom, who has always made me feel like a winner and that I can absolutely achieve anything that I set my mind to accomplish. You have taught me the true meaning of giving to give, and you lead by example, every day.

To Harvey Price, my dad, who was the most intelligent and generous man I ever met. I deeply regret that you passed away before SOC came into my life. I often think about the wonderful cards I would have sent you, or how you would have been proud to watch me develop as a businesswoman and entrepreneur. Dad, you are hugely loved and greatly missed.

To my brother, Marc Price, who has always set a high standard and been an example of excellence, leadership and innovation for others to follow.

To Annette Steiner, my grandmother, who is my most "mature retail customer" at the beautiful age of 93. You prove that anyone can and should use SendOutCards to be in better touch with the people they love!

To my uncles, aunts, cousins, and in-laws, for being so loving and supportive of my goals and dreams, and for providing great "card fodder" throughout the years! Though our family doesn't get together often, I've always appreciated how our love for each other is strong...and virtually drama-free!

To Christine Eisenman, for sending the birthday card and Starbucks gift card that forever changed my life.

To my fabulous Knights of the SOC Table, for your dedication, support, focus and leadership. I couldn't have done any of this without you! I am so fortunate to be able to share this wonderful journey with such special people.

To my incredible team, whose daily contributions, energies, and willingness to Listen to Life with SendOutCards Ears have enriched both my life and the lives of those around you.

To Kody Bateman, for creating a company with a powerful and loving reach, so that we may continually touch those around us in ways that we could never have imagined.

To Kathy Paauw and Judy O'Higgins, for your great upline leadership and source of ongoing support. Your team call where you interviewed me on March 1, 2010, was the main event that inspired me to finally put my magic sentences and nuggets into a book for others.

To Linda Larsen, for bringing her incredible wisdom, feedback and experience to the table. It is so exciting when you find people who share your joy and vision of all that this business and tool can be. Thank you Linda, for being a wonderful leader, motivator, collaborator, team member, Knight, and friend. And to the amazing Shivan Sarna and David Desrosiers for their feedback and insight, and John Scalzi for his never-ending support and humor...you all are the wind beneath my windsoc!

To Adam Packard, for your valuable and insightful feedback on my first version of this book. I deeply appreciate the care that you took to not only read it, but create those well thought-out suggestions that I took to heart.

To Jordan Adler, Jim Packard, DeMarr Zimmerman, David Frey, Megan Dresher, and Bob and Betty Ann Golden, for also taking the time to read my first draft, and for providing your most-valued comments and testimonials!

A huge thanks also to Bob and Betty Ann Golden, Jimmy Dick, Jeff Packard, Diane Walker, and all the other incredible leaders in SOC. You are an inspiration to us all, and we appreciate that you devote your time and energies to helping us all succeed in achieving our dreams.

To Sonie Lasker, my fabulous personal trainer and friend, for putting up with all those hours of me brainstorming about socks while we sweat, and for being an inspirational and helpful sounding board.

To Linda Seiden, my business coach, for helping me set my systems in place and my priorities in order, to allow my business to grow to the next level.

To Andre Panet-Raymond, my golf coach, for turning me into a pretty darned good golfer, giving me a reason to get away from my computer, and for providing great feedback on the first version of this book from a perspective outside the industry.

To SendOutCards (SOC), the incredible business opportunity that has given me the financial ability to be able to afford a personal trainer, a business coach and a golf teacher!

To Marci Marsh, Deepa Toomey, Rebecca Kloss, Monica Miller, Rachel Cohen, Margaretha Heidel, Beth Beyer, Bethany Gerber, Robin Fernandez, and many other wonderful friends, whose hilarious stories and experiences over the years have inspired the existence (and effectiveness!) of Jules Rules. Your support and friendship mean the world to me.

To Raoul Widman, my fearless illustrator, who was brave enough to go where no sock has gone before! Your talent and humor were invaluable during this project. Thanks for soldiering on despite the long hours, hard work, and impossibly short time span. I truly enjoyed bouncing ideas and working off of each other's creativity, to make these chapter titles come to life!

To Mary Ellen Motyl, Senior Manager and Knight, for being the originator of the follow-up binder system that I incorporated into my business and now so many others have adopted as well!

To Joel Eschenbach, my incredible web designer, who helped to create duplication and ease in my life.

To Denise Schweiger, for not hanging up on me, and recognizing how this system would be a great tool in your toolbox.

To Shawn Forno, for contributing his fun poem about missing socks. Little did you know that your musings would ever relate to anything in particular!

To Melody Marler Forshee at Eagle One Publishing, for all of your help in making my dream a reality.

To Sam Robinson, Joe Kenemore, Leann McFalls, Steve Diamond, Jeremy Diamond, Whitney Jensen, Paul Gerardis, Glen Bogue, Walter McFashion, Emily Robinson, Brandon Comstock, Cheryse Carhart, Jennifer Ollerton, Shua Moon, and many others at SOC Corporate, for your incredible help and support these last three years. You make SOC feel like a family instead of just a company, and I appreciate you all so much!

To all the New York City casting directors over the years, for making me strong in the face of rejection!

And finally, to everyone who has ever sent me inspirational, friendly and loving messages in cards, emails, and Facebook notes over the years. Your support, appreciation, and warmth are what make this business meaningful and dear to my heart. May this book, in some small way, help you all on your path to achieve greatness in your business and in your life.

ABOUT THE AUTHOR

Jules Price grew up in Montgomery Village, Maryland, outside of Washington, D.C. She earned a bachelor's degree in psychology and music from Connecticut College, and then moved to New York City to pursue her passion of singing and theater. She performed professionally for 12 years in musicals and operettas throughout New York City and various regional theaters around the country, including the National and International Tour of *The Sound of Music* as "Maria" throughout the U.S., Canada and Korea, and then understudied Marie Osmond in the role throughout Singapore, Bangkok, and Hong Kong.

In the fall of 2006, Jules and her husband, Jeremy Hammond-Chambers, chef/owner of Innovative Dining, a boutique private dining and catering company, moved to Sarasota, Florida. Jules was introduced to SendOutCards in 2007, when she received a birthday card and gift card from someone she'd never met. She instantly saw the value of the tool and the exciting opportunity it presented.

In addition to building her SOC business, she currently still sings with the New York City Ballet in *West Side Story Suites* and has traveled with them to New York City, Tokyo, Paris, London, Saratoga Springs, Washington, D.C., and Hong Kong.

Jules is now a corporate trainer, Eagle's Nest member and top producer in SendOutCards, and is passionate about helping others to "listen to life with SendOutCards ears" and achieve all the success they desire.

Secrets From the SOC Drawer

is also available as an eBook.

Visit www.eagleonepublishing.com for details.

EAGLE ONE
PUBLISHING
PO Box 26173
Salt Lake City, UT 84126
www.eagleonepublishing.com